REFLECTIONS
with Fr. Leo Clifford, O.F.M.

Father Leo Clifford, O.F.M.

EWTN Catholic Publishing

All Scripture references are taken from *The Holy Bible: Revised Standard Version*. San Francisco, Ignatius Press, 1966.

Nihil Obstat: Colin B. Donovan, S.T.L.
                              Birmingham, Alabama

Imprimatur: + Robert J. Baker, S.T.D.
                              Bishop of Birmingham in Alabama
                              Birmingham, Alabama
                              November 17, 2014

The Nihil Obstat and Imprimatur are official declarations that a book or pamphlet is free of doctrinal or moral error. No implication is contained therein that those who have granted the Nihil Obstat or Imprimatur agree with the contents, opinions or statements expressed.

Library of Congress Cataloging-in-Publication Data
Clifford, Leo, 1922-2012
Reflections with Fr. Leo Clifford, O.F.M.---1st ed.
p. cm.
1. Spiritual life—Catholic Church I. Clifford, Leo, 1922-2012. II. Title

Library of Congress Control Number: 2014921283

ISBN 978-1-940588-01-8

5817 Old Leeds Road, Irondale, Alabama 35210 USA
Tel.: 1.205.271.2900 • www.ewtn.com
Order copies through EWTN Religious Catalogue at www.ewtnrc.com

CONTENTS

REFLECTIONS I

Christianity

Some years ago, a book was published that was called *If I Could Preach Only Once*. It was a collection of essays by well-known lay people who, if they were given the chance to preach once in their lives, would preach on such-and-such a subject. And many of them chose Our Lady. It was a happy choice because with devotion to the Mother of God, she will see to it that we get our ship safely across the ocean of life to the Eternal Shore. Some said they would teach about a particular teaching of Our Lord and apply it to conditions in our world today; while others said that if they could preach but once in their lives, they would speak about the joys of Heaven as a help to our living on earth. Suppose you could preach once in your life. Suppose you were selected and put on one of those talk shows to tell the world what your religion means to you. What would you say? It would make an interesting survey, to find out what each of you would say. And as I am wondering about you, you have every right to wonder about me. If I could preach but once in my life, if this were the last sermon I were ever to preach, I would want to tell the whole world, as I want to tell you now, about the most fascinating and breathtaking truth in all Christ's teaching, that truth which is as

1

new as this morning's paper and as old as His sermon at the Last Supper, that truth which brings God down into the most amazing closeness to us, and lifts us up into the most frightening intimacy with Him. It is the mystery and the reality that Jesus Christ, the Son of God, the Second Person of the Blessed Trinity, is alive on earth at this moment in you and in me. The extraordinary words from St. John's Gospel, "I am the Vine; you are the branch. Live in me so that I, Your God, can live in you. If anyone loves me, the Father will love him, and we shall come to him and make our home in him. Unless you eat the flesh of the Son of Man and drink His blood, you shall not have life in you. He who eats my flesh and drinks my blood lives in me and I in him, and I shall raise him up on the last day" (John 15. 1,7-8). These are extraordinary words of our faith. Why did Christ found a Church? There is in Rome today the Holy Father surrounded by the College of Cardinals. There is the hierarchy of bishops, there is the priesthood, there is the Holy Sacrifice of the Mass, there are the Seven Sacraments, and there is the preaching of the Word of God, for only one reason. So that Jesus Christ could come live in you and in me. This is why He founded His Church. St. Francis said were he to meet a priest and an angel, he would first salute the priest and then the angel, because it is through the priest, however unworthy, however weak, however sinful he may be, that Christ chooses to come to us. When God created us, He created us unique. You and I inhabit our own silent world, the world of our thoughts and our fears and our dreams and our loneliness. Each one of us has our own peculiar twist of soul, our own fascination with evil that no one can see or understand. Each one of us has our own individual history. A unique destiny awaits each of us; one that we cannot share with any other human being. One day, you and I will die alone. We were born alone. And in the last analysis, however close we may be to our family and our friends, we inhabit our own silent world, alone. Into that aloneness, into that complexity, into that mystery that is you and I, Christ has come to live in the depth of our being, to share everything in our day. Claire Booth Luce was a convert to Catholicism. Her only child was killed in an accident and she was devastated. There was no reason to get up in the morning, now. Her life was plunged into utter darkness. Someone told her about Bishop Sheen. She went and she talked with him and she listened to him. And she was baptized a Catholic. A short time later, she went to The Catholic University in Washington and she stood there before the assembled student body and the faculty, and she said, "Would someone define a Catholic?" And she gave her own definition. She said, "A Catholic is someone to whom a stranger comes up in the street, merely to ask the time of day; the stranger should be able to tell from the tone of your voice, from the smile on your lips, from the gleam in your eye, that the Lord lives within you." This is the Good News! This is why He founded His Church. There is an old hymn that we sing in our churches in Ireland and that hymn says it all. "Be Thou my vision, O Lord of my heart. Not be all else to me save that Thou art. Thou, my best thought in the day or the night, waking or sleeping, Thy presence my Light. Riches I need not, nor man's empty praise. Thou, are My Inheritance through all my days; Thou and Thou only, the first in my heart. High King of Heaven, My Treasure Thou art."

Mercy of God

Even though we have never met, I know something very personal
about you. You are desperately searching for peace. We all of us
need peace for our soul as much as we need air for our body. We
cannot live without peace. We cannot even die without it. For, when
they finally put us in the grave, they will pray that we may rest in
peace. Peace is what was promised the night Our Lord was born.
"Glory to God in the highest," the angel sang, "and on Earth, peace
to men of goodwill." It was His own legacy when He was returning
to His Father. "My peace I leave with you. My peace I give to you."
It's that peace which surpasses all understanding, which the world
cannot give away. Peace is the fruit of the Holy Spirit's activity
in the Christian Soul - Love, Joy, Peace. Peace is the birthright of
every child of God. But look at all the Christians around us who
have no peace, and they have no peace because they do not know the
Lord. When you and I want to know the Lord, we dare not consult
our imagination, because it will play havoc with us. We go inside of
ourselves, and we find there all our limitations, all our peculiarities,
all our hang-ups, and we project them into a Supreme Being Whom
we call God, and we live out our lives in fear and trembling of Him,
and there is no such God. "I am thy Lord thy God. Thou shalt have
no strange Gods before Me." And look at all the strange gods so
many men and women worship – puny gods, tiny gods, vengeful
gods, and capricious gods – like themselves. When you and I want
to know the Lord, we have to go in faith to the Gospel and read what
is written there, and it will take all the faith that we have to accept
what is revealed in those Gospels. Our Lord, to aid our imagination,
went around telling stories to help us grasp something of the love,
mercy, and compassion of Our God. And the world loves the story

4

that He told of the Good Shepherd – God likening Himself to a shepherd of sheep, the Shepherd who knows each sheep by name, who loves the sheep, who's willing to lay down His life for the sheep. And one of those sheep gets tired of life in the fold, and He goes out in search of it, leaves the ninety-nine. And the Gospel tells us He goes on searching until He finds him. And when He does find him, there is no reproach, there is no reprimand, and there is no punishment. Rather does He put him on His shoulders, rejoicing, returning home with a song in His heart because He has found the sheep that was lost. This is so beautiful. Do you believe it? Because we don't understand it; we are not used to this kind of love. The only love you and I understand is the love the Irish poet wrote about when he said, " 'You gave me the key to your heart, my love; then why did you make me knock?' 'Oh, that was yesterday, saints above! And today I've changed the lock.' " And we understand only the love that promises eternal fidelity at the altar, and in two years is looking for a divorce. That is the only love that you and I are familiar with. But this unchanging love, this love that never wanes or never wavers, we have to accept this totally in faith. The Little Flower, that extraordinary French girl who died in a convent in Normandy at the age of twenty-four, tells us that if she had not become a saint – become a nun, rather – she would have become one of the great sinners of the world. She knew Him. She said, "Even though I should have every mortal sin in the world on my soul, I would still fling myself into the arms of His mercy, knowing that He loves me." Is this the God Whom you know? Whom I know? Our challenge is to believe what He has revealed. And so much for His theory; what was He like in practice? How did He treat sinners? Magdalene, whom respectable people avoided, her sins were taken away because she believed, because she loved. The thief on the cross, this man, after a lifetime of evil, who must have emptied many pockets as he broke many hearts, here he is being given Heaven in a moment by the grand and noble gesture by the God whose name is Love. Remember that same love and mercy and compassion and understanding is alive in the Church today with the same Lord, in the Sacrament of Reconciliation, the Sacrament of Penance, where you and I come with our sorrow and our sincerity. "And even though our sins be as red as scarlet, He will make our souls as white as snow." And when we tell the Lord our misgivings, we will hear from Him the loveliest words we shall ever hear this side of Paradise: "And I absolve you from your sins in the Name of the Father and of the Son and of the Holy Spirit." There is a poem written by an anonymous Christian that Malcolm Muggeridge called *The Kernel of Christianity*. It is Our Lord hanging on His Cross, speaking to Judas. Remember, Our Lord loved Judas and Judas once loved Him. And then he did the dastardliest deed in the history of our world – he sold His Lord for thirty pieces of silver. Here is the poem. "Judas, if true love never ceases, how could you, my friend, have come to this? To sell me for thirty silver pieces, betray me with a kiss? Judas, remember what I taught you. Do not despair while hanging on that rope. It's because you've sinned that I have sought you. I came to give you hope. Judas, let's pray and hang together, you on your halter, I upon my hill. Dear friend, even if you loved me never, you know I love you still."

The Holy Spirit

Who is the Holy Spirit? He is the Love of God. He is the Third
Person of the Blessed Trinity. He is the Father's Love for the Son
and the Son's Love for the Father. He is the Love that sent Our Lord
down here. He is the Love that brought Our Lord down here. He is
the Love that inspired His every thought, word and action. He is the
Love that took Him to Calvary to enable Him to give the last drop
of His Blood for you and me – the Breathtaking Love of God for us.
I don't have to remind you, my dear friends, that what inspires you
and me is not a book or a lecture or a sermon. No, what inspires
you and me is a person. We are attracted to a Person. A Person
fascinates us. A Person finally captivates us. And the Person is
Jesus Christ, alive on this Earth in the human beings whom He has
regenerated, who have been born-again into the life of the Blessed
Trinity. And my dear friends, when the Holy Spirit came to you and
me, He came with seven gifts – wisdom, understanding, counsel,
fortitude, knowledge, piety and the fear of the Lord. These seven
gifts are like the seven notes of music, which are destined to produce
a melody, the likes of which the world has never heard before. You
think of what Mozart and Chopin and Beethoven have done with
seven notes of music. And the melody you and I are destined to
produce on this earth, no one has ever heard before. You are to
become like Our Lord in a way St. Francis was never like Him, in
a way the Little Flower was never like Him. You are to show forth
something of the infinite beauty and radiance and love of the God
Who lives within you. And in the Fifth Chapter of St. Paul's Epistle
to the Galatians, we find the fruits of the Holy Spirit in the Christian
soul – love, joy, peace, patience, kindness, generosity, forbearance,
gentleness, faith, courtesy, temperateness, and self-control. And

against these, there is no law. Imagine encountering a human being who had these dazzling, intangible qualities in their soul – love, joy, peace, patience, kindness, and generosity. But you are to be that soul. You are to be this dazzlingly attractive radiant being on earth. St. Irenaeus said, "The glory of God is a human being radiantly alive – alive in the Spirit Whose Name is Love." Do you know that the Holy Spirit appeared five times on earth? As a dove at Our Lord's Baptism; as a cloud at the Transfiguration; as a breath when Our Lord says of the Apostles, breathing on them, "Receive the Holy Spirit. Whose sins you shall forgive, they are forgiven; whose sins you shall retain, they are retained." And He appeared as wind and as fire at Pentecost. And every morning at Mass, He comes five times. In the Penitential Rite, it is He who enables me to know my sinfulness. It is He who makes my failures clear to me. It is He who inspires my sorrow. He comes in the reading of the Scriptures. It was He who composed the Scriptures, and it is only He who will enable you and me to understand the deep, hidden meaning of the Scriptures. He comes in the Epiclesis, when the priest puts his hands over the paten and the chalice, and prays that the bread and wine may become the Body and Blood of Our Lord. He comes for the fourth time when we pray that we may be One Body, One Spirit in Christ. And He comes the fifth time in Holy Communion, because when Our Lord comes, the Father comes, and the Holy Spirit comes. He comes to make you and me what God intended before the stars were ever created in the sky – another Christ, alive in the 20th century. In the year of the Holy Spirit, the Holy Father asked us to be aware of Him, the Secret Guest of our soul. The great Belgian churchman, Cardinal Mercier, gave a secret of sanctity to his clergy. He said, "If for five minutes every day you withdraw into the sanctuary of your baptized soul, where the Spirit of Love lives, if you talk to Him there and listen to Him there," he said, "I guarantee you will pass through this world with great peace and tranquility and arrive at the gates of Paradise full of merit." G. K. Chesterton said that "Christianity has been found wanting, without having been tried." So many of us are not aware of the gift of God to us – the gift of love Who is within us to bring us alive in a way that will give glory to the Father. So, surely this ancient prayer is a prayer that finds an echo in our heart. "O God, You Who are Love, I pray You give me Love – Love in my thinking, love in my speaking, love in the secret recesses of my heart; love for those who are near and love for those who are far away; love for those with whom I work and love for those with whom I take my ease; love for those with whom I find it hard to bear, and love for those who find it hard to bear with me. And so, Lord, fill me with Your Love, that when I come to die, I may be worthy to spend my eternity with you who are Love."

Philosophy of Life

In the Tenth Chapter of St. Luke's Gospel, Our Lord tells us the most loved story in the world, the story of the *Good Samaritan*. And it came in answer to a lawyer's question, who asked Our Lord, "Who is my neighbor?" And instead of giving him a treatise on neighborly relations or some essay on sociology, He told him a story of a hundred and fifty words about a man who was left for dead on the side of the road. Two people passed by and ignored him, and one helped him. We can identify with the story very easily because we see ourselves in the story. Sometimes we are the one who is hurt; sometimes we are the one who goes by; and sometimes, hopefully, we are the one who helps. The story is also famous because it contains the three great philosophies of life by which we live. You say, "But I don't have a philosophy of life." We all do, consciously or unconsciously. The first philosophy is that of the robbers, which says, "What's yours is mine and I shall take it." This is the philosophy of bank robbers and petty thieves all over the world. In a more sophisticated way, it is the philosophy of the employer who defrauds his workers of an honest wage. He thinks their work belongs to him. And then it is the philosophy of the workers who take home a salary for eight hours solid work when they've done only seven hours of shoddy work. You see, because we are sinners, the greed and the selfishness is in all of us, and we want to grasp. We have to be so careful. And then there is the philosophy of the priest and the Levite, which says, "What is mine is mine and I shall keep it." It is hard to blame them. They didn't cause the man any injury. They were innocent bystanders. Maybe they had a bus to catch. Maybe they had an appointment with the doctor and time is precious. So, we make allowances for them as we make allowances for ourselves. But, my dear friends, we forget; nothing is ours. Everything we have, we have received – everything, to the next minute, the next breath we draw – all gifts of God. Sadly, we become so enamored with His gifts, we do not possess them; they possess us, and we become slaves to the gifts of our God, because we are blinded by the sinfulness within us. And then there is the philosophy of the Samaritan. It is interesting that Our Lord does not call him "good." Neither does St. Luke. He's called the "good Samaritan" by the world because his is the philosophy that should be ours: "What is mine is yours, and I shall share it." This is what Our Lord taught us – to give our cloak as well as our coat, to go the extra mile; to forgive not seven times, but seventy times seven times;

not to refuse him who wants to borrow from us. This is the Christian philosophy by which you and I must strive to live. I know it is not easy. I know we have to begin again each day. I know the struggle is real. But we are not alone in the battle. The Lord Himself, Who gave the philosophy, is within us to enable us to achieve success. And Our Lord is not talking only about monetary problems. We may not have much to give, but we have a kind word, a smile, and a listening ear. We can make a phone call; we can visit a sick neighbor; we can go to the hospital; we can write a letter. What do we do with the love that God pours forth into your heart and mine, the love that is in us now, in every one of us, as His child? By definition, you cannot keep love. Love must be given away. You cannot buy love; you cannot barter it; you cannot sell it; you cannot store it. You can only give it away. "A song is not a song until it is sung. A bell is not a bell until it is rung. And love is not love until it is given away," to you. I have Our Lord's own love, and He's depending on me to give it back to those around me, because while you and I are alive, He is alive. And surely, the prayer of St. Francis is our prayer. "Lord, make me an instrument of your peace. Where there is darkness, let me bring your light. Where there is despair, let me bring your hope. Where there is anger and hatred and confusion and turmoil, let me bring your love. Let me be your child, truly."

Forgiveness

In the Eighteenth Chapter of St. Matthew's Gospel, we find St. Peter speaking a language that we understand, we who are small-minded, calculating, selfish people. He comes to Our Lord and says, "How often should I forgive my brother, seven times?" Now that's very generous. Not three times, not even double it, but seven times. Who could be more generous than that? And Our Lord said, "No, not seven times. Seventy times seven times." And then Our Lord told the story of a man who owed something and was forgiven. He then found a friend who owed him a little and he demanded the last penny and had the man thrown in jail. We need to be reminded that as long as we are on this earth, we are in God's debt. We are always needing His forgiveness, always needing His understanding, always needing His mercy and His love. If Christianity means that Christ comes to live in you and me, to share our lives and to give us the secret of radiance, and He gives us His own love to fashion and form and mold us into children of the Father, not in word and in tongue, but in deed and in very truth...If this is our religion and our faith, then surely we must admit how abysmally we've failed. We forget Him; we neglect Him; we ignore Him. We are preoccupied with ourselves, our health, our happiness, our well-being, our future, our friends. We forget the Lord. And we fall so much in love with His gifts that we forget Him, the Giver. The Lord comes to live in me and possess me. This is our faith. The poet expressed the problem very wonderfully when he said, "If thou could empty all thyself of self, like to a shell uninhabited, then coming might He find thee on the ocean shelf and say, 'This is not dead,' and fill thee with Himself instead. But thou art replete with very thou and hath such rude activity that when He comes He says, 'This is enough unto itself, 'twere better let it be. It is so small and full, there is no room for me.'" That's the tragedy of our lives. "I know better than the Lord the things that are to my peace. I know how I ought to live; I who am small and smug and self-satisfied." But the truth is, if we behave like this, and so often we do, we are stunted in our growth. We are spiritual pygmies. We are crawling on the face of the earth when we are destined to be flying into the face of the sun. But there is another aspect to this. If I do not forgive those who hurt me, if I have no forgiveness for those who have offended me, then I am less mature than I should be, less free than I should be. Indeed, I become a slave. Have you ever met someone who was unforgiving, who became hard and bitter with a closed mind? Then you've met someone who is incarcerated by their own choosing, and thrown the key away. I remember many years ago, preaching at a funeral of an old, old man. And it was very difficult because there was an old man in the front pew who cried from his heart all during Mass. At the end of Mass, I went to speak to him and I said, "Was the man who died your friend?" He said, "Father, he was my brother. He was my only brother and we have not spoken for fifty years. And I was always coming to tell him I was sorry. I was always going to ask his forgiveness. I was always going to visit him but I never did. And now it's too late. And from beyond the grave I want him to forgive me, and I want My God to forgive me." And I said to him, "What was the problem? What was the difficulty you had?" He said, "I have forgotten." How sad! How tragic! All those years he was carrying this heavy load, this burden, because he never came to ask forgiveness. In Ireland, we used to say that we were willing to bury the hatchet but we made sure to mark the spot because we might need it again. Oh, no! That cannot be! We must go and find a deep river or a lake or the ocean and stand there and throw it in over our shoulders and forget it; otherwise, we will not be children of God, as we are destined to be. Do we ever stop to think of what we say every day in the prayer Our Lord taught us? "Forgive us our trespasses as we forgive those who trespass against us." In effect I'm saying, "Lord, You see the way I treat those who have hurt me. You see my understanding, my generosity,

13

my compassion, and my genuine forgiveness. That's the way you must treat me." My dear friends, if you and I, as a child of God, are destined on this earth to show forth His forgiveness, His love, His compassion, His mercy to the human beings around us, then we must go on striving every day to meet His standards and live by His ideals. And surely this is a prayer that finds an echo in our hearts. "Oh, Lord, please teach me to forgive. As I come out of my darkness and my loneliness and my selfishness, help me to share with others and never grow weary of sharing the forgiveness and the love that you are forever giving to me."

Our Lady

Ralph Waldo Emerson tells the story of a journey through the States in a coach. It was a day in which the clouds were low and heavily charged, and the people in that coach were silent, preoccupied and sad, as they went on their journey. Here and there the coach stopped. At one place, a young woman got in carrying her baby in her arms. She was tall and radiant and beautiful. And they continued on their journey. But somehow, something happened. It seemed as if the atmosphere was completely changed. The people were chatting animatedly, one with another, now, all because of the advent of this unknown woman and her child into their lives. We, too, are on a journey, down here in this valley of tears; and there is a woman and her child in our lives, too. But we know who She is – Mary, our life, our sweetness, and our hope. The Vatican Council reminds us that Our Lady must be in our lives under two headings – as our mother and as our model. She's your mother and mine, far more truly than that being on earth whom we call "Mother." For if, at this moment, you are alive with God's own life, if there is now coursing through your veins and beating next to your heart something of the unending life of the Blessed Trinity, if Christ is being formed in you, if there is in you that grace that will one day blossom into glory, it is all because Our Lady said, "Yes" to God when He asked Her if She would be the channel through which He would come and live in you. She is the mother of the Christ who is to be formed in you and me. And we need our mother to help us do the great work that is our challenge in life. And She's our model in faith. St. Augustine reminds us that Our Lady was the first disciple, and that she brought Christ alive by faith in her soul long before She brought Him alive in Her body. When Our Lady said to the Angel, "Be it done unto me according to Thy word," She set out on the greatest adventure possible for a human being. She gave God a blank check on Her life. No more questions would be asked. She believed that He was her Father; that He loved Her, that she was His child, and that she would accept whatever He arranged. Well, my dear friends, you don't need to have much imagination to imagine Our Lady in the seventh month, the eighth month, the ninth month, with life stirring within Her. As like all mothers-to-be, She was crocheting and knitting and preparing for the birth of the child. And then one morning, a selfish, moody, compulsive man who had authority from God, decided that his people should be enrolled. Joseph would go and do his duty; Mary would go with him. They arrived in the crowded city. Every door is closed; every face is hard. There is no room for them at the inn. They have to go into a stable to bring forth the Child. You know what the Franciscans have done with the crib. It is so romantic; it is so inspiring. What was the reality? Put yourself in Our Lady's place. Where is the angel now? Where is God now? Was she forgotten, neglected, and abandoned because she had to bring forth a Child in a stable? It did not make sense. But she believed. Isn't that our problem? We always want things to make sense in our terms. We have to understand; we have to be able to fathom; we have to be on top of every situation. Our Lady is our model in faith; in accepting by faith what she could not understand. Well, she was about over that shock when she got in for another one. She had to take the Child to Egypt. If there was a bad word for the Jews, it was "Egypt," because She knew what God had to do to get His people out of Egypt. And now send them back into Egypt? It doesn't make sense by our sophisticated standards. And she went; and she stayed; and she returned when the angel told Joseph, "to Nazareth." And she saw Him grow up through the difficult years of adolescence. She saw Him become twenty-five, she saw Him become thirty, doing nothing for the salvation of the world by our standards. And then He went out and surrounded Himself with people who did not understand Him; people who were obtuse, selfish, unthinking and ambitious. At the end, one of them betrayed Him and died in despair at his own hand; another one denied Him and the rest ran away and left Him to die alone. The Fathers of the Church tell us, on that Friday men call "Good," Mary was the only human being on earth who believed as she stood at the foot of the cross, that this wreck of humanity dying of a broken heart was God Almighty, dying for the salvation of us all. My dear friends, we need Our Lady to teach us how to believe every day, how to accept what we cannot understand, how to allow God to have His way with us, and how to believe, as she believed, that His love is the great reality, the unchanging factor in our lives, always, always, always. And surely, the prayer of the great St. Bernard is our prayer today. "Remember, O most gracious Virgin Mary, that never was it known that anyone who fled to Thy protection, implored Thy help, or sought Thy intercession was left unaided." Never was it known. "Inspired by this confidence, I fly unto You, O Virgin of Virgins, My Mother. To You I come, before You I stand, sinful and sorrowful. O Mother of the Word Incarnate, despise not my petitions, but in your mercy, hear and answer me."

Prayer

I am going to try to talk to you about the most personal, mysterious, and incommunicable thing about you – your relationship with God in prayer. Prayer is defined as the elevation of the mind and heart to God. You remember that from your catechism. But it is the elevation of my mind and my heart to My God. And where is He? Everywhere. "In Him I move and breathe and have my being. I am in the midst of Him as a bird is in the air, as a fish is in the sea. His Ear is always lying close to my lips, even while I sleep and dream." But now, because you and I are His children, grafted onto His Son, Christ, regenerated by the waters of Baptism, He is living in the depths of our soul, nearer to us than we are to ourselves. And we must discover Him there in faith and make Him real. The Bible is filled with the reality of God. In the Book of Genesis, how real He was for Adam and Eve. We are told, "They walked with God in the afternoon air, in the cool of the evening, in the Garden." How real He was for Enoch, who walked with God and was seen no more by men. How real He was for Moses, who spoke to God as a friend speaks to a friend. Moses said to God, "Show me Your Face." And God said, "No man can see My Face and live, but you will catch a glimpse of me as I pass by." And Moses went into the cleft of the rock, and as the Lord went by, he cried out, "Ah, the Lord God. The

Lord God!" How real He was for Isaiah, the man of unclean lips. He had a vision of the Deity and he heard Him say, "Whom shall I send?" And Isaiah said, "Here I am. Send me." How real He was for David. "The Lord is my Shepherd. There is nothing I shall want." "The Lord is the light of my countenance. Of whom should I be afraid? Though I walk in the valley of death, I need fear no evil, because you are with me." How real He was for Jeremiah. "Lord, You seduced me; but I allowed you to seduce me." He was so real for all the prophets and all the judges and the entire noble men and women in the Old Testament. And we turn the pages of the New Testament, and we find God walking the dusty roads of our Earth in Jesus Christ. And the saints are the men and women for whom Our Lord has become real. How real He was for St. Francis. "Lord, two graces I ask of You before I die – that I may experience in my body something of the suffering that You endured for love of us; and that I may experience in my soul something of the love that caused You to suffer." How real He was for the Dominican laywoman, St. Catherine of Siena. "All the way to Heaven is Heaven," she said, "because of Him Who is the Way living in me." How real He was for the great Spanish mystic, St. Teresa of Avila. "Let nothing disturb you; let nothing frighten you. All things are passing. God alone is changeless. And he who has God wants nothing." How real He was for the Irish poet Joseph Mary Plunkett. "I see His Blood upon the rose; and in the stars, the glory of His Eyes. His body gleams amid eternal snows; His tears fall from the skies. I see His face in every flower. The thunder and the singing of the birds are but His Voice. Carven by His power, rocks are His written words. All pathways by His feet are worn. His strong heart stirs the ever-beating sea. His crown of thorns is twined with every thorn; His

Cross is every tree." Good for them! How about you and me? As we go on our unremembered way down here in this valley of tears, how real has the Lord become for you and me? Have we discovered Him to be what He is – Our changeless friend, the companion of our exile, the lover of our soul, Our Father and Our God? Surely, if you and I believe what we say we believe, we cannot begin a day without some thought of Him. The new day, freshly minted from His Hand, in love, to you and me, given us so that we may discover Him. And He's in us, wanting to share all the trivia of our waking hours, wanting to be part of everything. Is there something in your day or mine from which He is to be excluded? You remember the lovely story of St. Charles Borromeo, who loved to play cards. One day he was absorbed in his game of cards when someone nearby said to him, "What would you do if Gabriel were to sound the last trumpet now?" He said, "I would go on playing cards," because he was playing cards with the Lord. Is there something in your day or mine from which He is excluded? You know, Our Lord was born in a stable. A stable is a place that stinks, a stench we don't like. We pretend it isn't there. He wants to be born in that part of you and me that we are ashamed of – that shameful, sinful, sordid part of our lives. He is not to be excluded from that. Surely, my dear friends, this is the prayer that finds an echo in our hearts. "Oh Lord, You Who have prepared a place for my soul; prepare my soul for that place. Prepare it with faith and longing and love, and help me never to forget as I wander here in this valley of tears that my destiny is to be with You and the Father and the Holy Spirit in the glory that lasts forever and forever."

Hope

Did you ever stop to think that God never had to create you? Never! Millions of possible human beings whom God saw when He created you, he left to remain in their nothingness, and they might have worshipped Him a thousand times better than you will ever worship Him. They might have been higher, holier, far more interesting. But He did not create them. There was some nameless thing about you, which attracted Him. It was you with your single, unmated soul, which in the calmness of His eternal wisdom and love drew Him to create you. This is our faith. And the love that took you out of nothingness in the yesteryears has not abandoned you. He did not turn you into this world and leave you here on your own to sink or swim. That love has enveloped you and sustained you every moment since then, and it is enveloping you and sustaining you now. The next breath you and I draw, the next beat of our heart, is an act of God's love for us. Were God to cease to love you for one instant, you would cease to be. We did not make ourselves; neither can we manage ourselves. We are totally dependent on Our God. Surely, my dear friends, it is logical that we ought to trust Our God. St. Augustine said, "The soul that is not alive with hope, as well as with faith and love, is not complete." Have you made an "Act of Hope" recently? "Oh, My God, I hope in You for grace in this life and for glory in the life to come, because You promised it; and unlike us, You never go back on Your word, You never break Your promise. And I hope in You, O God, because of Your mercy, which is above all of Your works, which is not put off by my failure, by my stupidity, by my sins. And I hope in You, O God, because of your power, which is all mighty and can do all things, even with me. Therefore, O God, My Father, I, Your creature and your child, trust you." My dear friends, the supernatural virtue of hope is hard work. You know, Our Lord came here to show us how to live, and His standards are so different from ours. He spent thirty of His thirty-three years in a remote corner of an obscure land. His life was unseen, unknown, and unrecorded. He came to show us how to live. With thirty years of unrecorded activity, to our standards, a whole generation steeped in heathenism and the worship of false gods, while Our Lord sawed and planed wood in a carpenter's shop. It doesn't make sense. We think of what men and women have done in thirty years. Between the age of thirty and thirty-three, Alexander the Great had conquered the East. At twenty-eight, Napoleon was a world power, feared and respected. At twenty-two, William Pitt was Prime Minister of England. And at the age of thirty, Our Lord had done nothing in the world's eyes. But, my dear friends, those hidden years in Nazareth have sent the saints into ecstasy. Our Lord chose to live a life of work and monotony and drudgery and boredom and labor; and to be the object of injustice and ingratitude and superficiality and casualness and indifference because that would be your lot and mine. He already lived our lives in love for us, and He's in us now, to enable you and me to meet the challenge of each hour. In the Third Chapter of St. Paul's Letter to the Ephesians there are the extraordinary words that ought to be written down in gold because gold does not tarnish. "He whose power is at work in you is powerful enough and more than powerful enough to achieve His designs, beyond all your hopes and your dreams." He has a design for you, for me. We must believe in Him; we must trust Him. You remember what Mother Teresa said, how to make God laugh? Bring Him your own designs, your own plans. Why? Because our plans are full of flaws and imperfections; for our blinded eyes cannot see beyond the present moment. The God Who made us sees into eternity, and His plan for you and for me is filled with love. St. Claude de la Colombière, who was the spiritual director of St. Margaret Mary, said, "Lord, I may fail in life. I may lose your grace by sin. But I shall never lose my hope. And when I am dying, not all the demons in hell will be able to tear it away from me." The cry is made to all Christians, "You shall not despair." Of all the sins that you and I could commit, despair is the most mischievous, the most paralyzing of effort, because there is no soul this side of the grave beyond redemption – no soul. There is no one, howsoever tortured and twisted, who cannot be filled with God's own peace. There is no one howsoever low who cannot be lifted to the greatest heights by God's power. Therefore, you and I must hope in Him.

Faith

The Irish playwright George Bernard Shaw wrote a play called *Pygmalion*. It was set to music and known to the world as *My Fair Lady*, and it was really an event in the theatre. It's a very simple story. It's a story of a girl selling flowers at a street corner in London one night when people were coming out from the opera at Covent Garden. And a man, who was an authority on speech, hearing this girl emit such ugly sounds, put on a wager with his friend. And he said, "If only I could teach her elocution, I guarantee in six months I could pass her off as a duchess." In the story, Eliza Doolittle comes to Professor Higgins for lessons in speech. And at the end of six months, she is the "fair lady" of British society. That's the story. Wherein lies its power, its charm? Why are people there in the theatre night after night, enchanted as they watch the story of Eliza unfold before their eyes? Because, my dear friends, there is in every human heart the secret longing and wish and dream and desire that the impossible will happen for it, too. That one day, like Eliza, it will be taken out of the rut in which it is living and placed on a pedestal – that one day the castle in Spain will become a reality. Haven't you dreamed like that? Haven't I? But for us, the dream has come true. We could not be higher, greater, and nobler. We are one with God Himself. On the day of our Baptism, we were lifted out of the rut of our creature-hood and brought up to the level of God Almighty, made His child in very truth. In the words of St. Peter, "We became partakers of the Divine Nature, sharing God's Own Unending Life" (2 Pet. 1:4). And on that day when the saving waters of Baptism were poured on our heads, we were given the extraordinary gift of faith; to have a relationship with God, which is the most solid and lasting and satisfying experience in the whole world. Now, when we were created, we were given three great urges – needs, proclivities, demands, call them what you will – that must be satisfied if we are going to live sane lives. And we can satisfy these needs either on a natural or a supernatural plane. The first and strongest is for life. We are madly in love with life. Nobody wants to die! We believe everything the doctor tells us. We take the cough drops and we have the injections and we go on a diet because the doctor says it. And what are we trying to achieve? To prolong by a year, or two or three, a life that is already doomed. Now don't you and I say we believe, we have within us a life that will never die, God's own life? How much time and thought and energy do we expend on that? And then the second great need that we have is for knowledge. Man is defined as a curious animal. I want to know, and I want to know more. I have to have the morning paper and the evening news, and I must read the latest novel. St. Paul boasted, "I know nothing but Christ, and Him crucified." Do you and I know Christ? Oh, we know about Him. We know what saints have said about Him. We know what preachers say in the pulpit about Him. But knowing about Him and knowing Him are two entirely different things. I could take you into a library where there are books on swimming. You could read the books and write a brilliant paper on swimming. I could bring you to a pool and have an Olympic star amaze you with his prowess in the water. But you would never swim by reading a book or by watching somebody else swim. Never would you swim until you went into the water yourself, alone, and discovered it has the power to uphold you. And you will never know the Lord merely by listening to what somebody says or by reading what somebody wrote. Never until you use the faith He gave you at baptism and go on searching for Him until you find Him in the darkness of your own soul, where He lives, where you will taste and see that the Lord is sweet. And the great need we have for love. We want to love and to be loved. This is the way God made us. And so, we have the friends who flatter us; and so there are the niches we fill in society, which make us feel wanted, accepted. We remember people at Christmas with a card and we try to remember their birthdays. That is all very wonderful on the lower level, but the other level? St. Paul tells us: "I live in the faith of the Son of God, Who loved me and delivered Himself for me." But you and I must believe in faith that God is madly in love with us at every moment of the day and night, with a love that never wavers, never wanes; a love that is unchanging, a love that is eternal. Our Lord told us that we must become perfect, as our Heavenly Father is perfect. How does God the Father find His perfection at this moment in Heaven? He does so in knowing Christ, in loving Him and in being loved by Him. The bond of their love is the Holy Spirit who dwells within. It is when I know the Lord living in me and I know that He loves me and that I am trying to love Him in return, then I begin to experience a happiness, a serenity, a fulfillment, a peace that belongs to God alone. And so, my dear friends, this little prayer from the French will find an echo in your heart. "Oh Lord, I thank you for loving me; and I shall not cry out to you that I am not worthy, because that you should love me, sinner that I am, is an act worthy of You, Who are Love Itself. Oh Lord, I thank you for loving me."

Charity

Do you remember how the fairy tales ended when we were children and we used to sit there, wide-eyed and open-mouthed, waiting for the end of the story? That man dressed in rags at whom the poor people threw their food, he turned out to be their king. The king went round among his people disguised as a beggar. If they were kind to him, he gave them half his kingdom; if they were unkind to him, he placed them in a cauldron of boiling oil. Now, this theme of mistaken identity has inspired the great stories of the world. A woman risks her life to save a child, her own daughter. The doctor at the end of the day, weary from work and very much in need of sleep, decides he will do the emergency surgery that has just come in – his own son, brought in from an accident. And of course, this has been the spice of the literary life. The first great play ever written was the Greek play, *Oedipus Rex,* in which the family did not recognize each other until the final scene. In Shakespeare's *The Comedy of Errors,* the whole comedy revolves round the mistaken identity of two sets of twins. And you remember, in his *The Merchant of Venice*, Portia is so disguised in the robes of a lawyer that no one recognizes her. Now, there is one story of mistaken identity that we need to be reminded of. St. Paul gives us the shock ending of the greatest story ever told in the Twenty-Fifth Chapter of St. Matthew's Gospel. "And then the King shall come in the clouds of Heaven with great power and majesty, and all His angels with Him. And He shall separate the good from the bad, putting the good on His right and the wicked on His left. And to the good He will say, 'Come, you blessed of My Father. Possess the Kingdom prepared for you from the foundation of the world, because I was hungry, and you gave me to eat; I was thirsty and you gave me to drink; I was sick and in prison, you visited me; naked and you clothed me; I was a stranger and you took me in" (Matt. 25:31-38). And then we shall say to Him, you and I, because we shall be there, "Lord, when did I see you? I lived my days and nights under the friendly skies of the United States. I never saw you. Where were you?" And then will come the greatest revelation of all time, as Christ will look into your eyes and mine, and utter these words: "Amen, amen, I say to you, 'What you did to those around you, you did to Me.' " "What you did to those around you, you did to Me." So, my dear friends, there is no escaping the logic that our every thought, word and deed to our neighbor is to Our Lord. And our thoughts – what a vast, thickly populated world our mind is. And what a very unkind world it can be. I so easily push God off His Judgment Seat, and I sit there pronouncing on others, though I have neither the knowledge nor the authority to judge anyone. Never in my life have I seen a motive. I see an action; but I have no idea what inspires that action. Suppose you and I had lived in Nazareth some months after the Angel Gabriel had appeared and seen this lovely teenage girl become pregnant before she was married. Don't you think we would have judged? Our Lady was judged by the village gossips. The evidence was before their eyes. Suppose we had lived in Magdala and seen the other Mary come up the street. Wouldn't we have avoided her like the plague – that wicked woman! How could we have known her potential for greatness, her real love for Our Lord? Suppose in the Middle Ages, we had lived in Italy, in Cortona, and St. Margaret lived with a man to whom she was not married. Wouldn't we have thundered against her from our pulpits? She is what you and I will never be – a canonized saint. What are we going to do with our mind, so small, so ignoble, so unlike the mind of Christ? We can't take it to Heaven. There's nothing there but love. And we'll not leave it behind simply because we close our eyes in death. Oh no, it will have to be burnt out of us slowly, in the heats of Purgatory. And our words – oh what power we have with our tongues to bless and to curse; to make people happy and to make them miserable. How often we slash Christ, far worse than the soldiers ever did at the pillar, with the haughty, unkind, sarcastic things we say. Every idle word that man speaks, he shall have to render an account for it. When Our Lord told us that "not on bread alone does man live," He was reminding us that men and women have souls as well as bodies. The needs of the soul are far greater than the needs of the body. For every thousand men and women in the world today who can mend a broken leg, there isn't one who can mend a broken heart. And broken hearts are all around us. And they can be healed only by the kindness and the love that you and I who say we believe have to give. What are our deeds? What we do for those around us? In the lovely legend of St. Martin of Tours, he meets a beggar man who asks him for alms. He has nothing to give, so he tears his cloak in two and shares it with him. That night, the beggar appeared to him. It was Our Lord. St. Francis kissed a leper, the most difficult thing he could do.

His sensitive nature shrank from those creatures. When he turned round, there was nobody there. And there began the world's most lovely and most lyrical sanctity, because Francis knew he had kissed Christ. Do you know the Chinese definition of hell? Sitting at a gourmet banquet, with the table filled with all kinds of delights, but the chopsticks are so long, I cannot get the food in my mouth. What was their idea of Heaven? The same banquet, the same table, but I am feeding my neighbor across the table. Surely, the prayer of St. Ignatius is our prayer. "Teach me, My God, to be generous. Teach me to love and serve you as you deserve, to give and not to count the cost, to fight and not to heed the wounds, to toil and not to seek for rest, to labor and to look for no reward except your love."

Holy Communion

On any given morning when you and I come to Mass and offer ourselves to Our Lord as He presents us to the Father, what happens? In return, He gives Himself to us. And only I know how small and mean and miserable and selfish I am, the gift of me. No wonder the Church cries out, *"O Admirabile Commercium!"* which means "O wonderful exchange!" In return for me, I receive into my soul the All-Holy, All Pure, and All-Loving God, for whom the Angels veil their faces. When John Henry Newman, in his Oxford days, was thinking of joining the Church, word got out among his friends and they tried so hard to dissuade him. They said, "If you become a Catholic, you can never set foot on this campus again where you are so loved." He said, "I know, but I must become a Catholic." They said to him, "Do you realize, with your genius for friendship, you will lose all your friends? None of us will ever speak to you again." He said, "I know. I know very well, but I must become a Catholic."

Finally, they said to him, "Do you realize that if you take this step, you will lose your income, $75,000 a year?" He looked up at them and said, "$75,000 a year? What is it to one Holy Communion?" Because, my dear friends, one Holy Communion is enough to make a saint. When the Lord comes to you and me, He communicates all of His loveliness to us so that we may use it and be a witness to Him in the darkness of this world. Our God descends to our level in order to lift us up to His, so that we will become what He is. And He is Love. So we are to be changed into Love. Now, love is not something vague or ethereal or intangible. St. Paul analyzes it so clearly in his Thirteenth Chapter of First Corinthians. "Love is patient; love is kind; it feels no envy. It is never perverse or proud. It does not brood over an injury. It takes no pleasure in wrongdoing but it rejoices at the victory of truth. It sustains, it hopes, it endures to the end." This is a description of Our Lord. It's a description of you and me. How patient are you? Oh, of course, you're patient. You're civilized; you're disciplined. But is your patience something that is limited and calculated? My dear friends, that is sheer unadulterated paganism. The pagans behaved like that. You and I must have the patience of Our Lord, who was lied about, treated unjustly, spat upon, and led to His Death without opening His Mouth. And He communicates that patience to you and to me in Holy Communion. Do we use it? Or is that patience of the Lord there in the depths of your being and mine, unused? And how kind are we? Oh yes, we are kind to certain people; others, we ignore. But our kindness depends on our health or on our mood or on the time of day. In the morning, early, before coffee, we're not too kind. But, so do the pagans behave. Ours must be the kindness of Christ, Who was kind to sinners who hated Him, Who was kind to children who can be so exasperating, kind to their mothers who can be unreasonable, kind to the sick, who can be so demanding. He was always kind. St. Vincent DePaul gives one formula for sanctity – "Be kind. Be kind and you will be a saint." That sounds easy. Oh, my dear friends, to be kind to the stupid and the arrogant and the proud and the selfish and the ungrateful, to those who squander my kindness and never say thank you and come back for more – to be kind to them, I need to be dead to myself and alive to the Lord. My dear friend, the secret is to keep our eyes riveted on Christ. We will change and we will become like Him and we will never know it. We're not supposed to know it. He will know it. And the Father will be given glory. Your great American writer, Nathaniel Hawthorne, tells the lovely story of the boy who lived in a village. And across from the village was the mountain in which he saw so clearly the features of a human being. And he was always looking at the mountain, wondering whose face it was. He looked at everyone in the village, but no one resembled the face in the mountain. Whenever a stranger came to town, he ran up and looked at them, but they didn't resemble the face in the mountain. Finally, the story ends by telling us that as the boy grew into manhood, he himself became the face in the mountain. Wouldn't it be wonderful if you and I gazed at Our Lord so long and so lovingly that people could say of us, as they said of Peter, "Thou also art with Jesus of Nazareth, thy very speech betrays thee." Well, this is our prayer – that at the end of our days on this earth, we may be changed truly into the God whose name is Love.

The Mass

I'm going to try to talk to you about what the Second Vatican Council calls "the source and summit of our religion," the Holy Sacrifice of the Mass. And how I wish I had the intelligence of an archangel, so that I could inspire you and myself with love for this central act of worship of our religion, this mystery of faith where our brilliant intelligence isn't much good to us, where our emotions come in the way, where our senses bog us down, where you and I are as children before Our God, accepting in faith what He said and what His Church teaches. When we talk about the Holy Sacrifice of the Mass, we have to think about time and eternity. Here we are living in time, you and I. Yesterday is gone; we are waiting for tomorrow; and the present moment eludes us even as we try to grasp it. The moment in which you turned on your television set is gone forever. God lives in eternity; where there is no yesterday, where there is no tomorrow. God is not waiting for the sunset or the dawn. God lives in the eternal "now," where there is neither past nor future. God sees you and me at this moment, not just as we are now; but already dead and buried, and judged and safely home with Him forever with life behind us. This God sees now; as you and I are here, worrying and fretting about a future that may never come. It makes us dizzy even to think about it. Now, God came out of eternity into time. "The Word was made flesh and dwelt among us." God, the Creator of Heaven and Earth, became a human being. That Baby lying in the straw, needing the care and love of a mother was a baby like any other, but He was God Almighty and His wisdom was ruling the world. That boy who kicked a ball on the village green, who went on an errand for His Mother, who went to bed and left the day behind was a little boy, like any other little boy; but He was the Creator of Heaven and Earth. On that Friday men call "Good," He died. There were three crosses there against a darkened sky. This has been recorded by friends and by enemies. But the Man on the center cross was God and no one was taking His life away from Him. Freely He was laying it down as a sacrifice of love to the Father, and it is there, enduring outside of time, if only you and I could find it. And that is precisely the miracle and the mystery of the Mass: That any validly ordained priest has the power, from God Himself, to bring alive in our midst the greatest moment in the history of our world. When we come to talk about the Holy Sacrifice of the Mass, we have to talk about symbols. Now, a symbol is an external expression of something that is internal. We live by symbols, you and I. The poet John Donne was not quite right when he said, "No man is an island." Everyone is an island. You remember Helen Keller. She could not communicate. She was marooned on her island until Annie Sullivan persevered to get her to communicate. Words are symbols. The words that I utter, the sounds that come from me, you understand, and they produce a link between us. A smile is a symbol. Not a word is uttered, but a smile conveys a world of love and happiness and gratitude. A handshake is a symbol. I extend my hand to you, my fellow traveller on the way home to God. Now, the liturgy is full of symbols – the altar, the steps of the altar, the altar-cloth, the flowers, the vestments – they are all conveying a meaning, an inner meaning. One of the loveliest symbols in the liturgy, for you and me, is the little drop of water that is plunged into the wine at the Offertory. The priest puts wine into the chalice. It symbolizes the strong, life-giving Christ; and then, one drop of water, weak, insignificant, hardly noticeable – you and me. And that little drop of water is mingled with the wine, becomes part of the wine, is no longer distinguishable from the wine, and at the Consecration becomes changed into Our Lord. And you and I come to Mass, come to Calvary with our sorrows and our sins and our failures and our spiritual ambitions and our fitful attempts at love. And Our Lord takes them and makes them part of Himself, and He offers them to the Father. And you and I, weak, insignificant human beings, through Him, our Elder Brother, are able to penetrate the very scars and give God Almighty glory and praise that is infinite, thanksgiving that is infinite, reparation not only for my own sins, but the sins of a million worlds. And I am able, through My Elder Brother, His Beloved Son, to ask anything in His Name. It is an extraordinary mystery. It is our privilege. No wonder the Council reminds us, "It is the source and summit of our Christian lives." Surely, this ancient prayer will find an echo in your hearts today. "Oh, Lord, I confess that there is within me so much that is ignoble, selfish and sinful. My little house is in ruins. I cannot repair it. You yourself must come to rebuild it so that it may be a fit dwelling for you all the days of my life on Earth."

REFLECTIONS II

Humility

Did you ever stop to think that the only thing Our Lord asked us to learn of was humility? "Learn of me for I am meek and humble of heart and you will find rest for your souls." But you and I, who listen to the father of lies so easily, imagine we will find what we crave in flattery, in the applause of the crowd, in riches. But what is humility? What is this vague, ethereal, intangible, supernatural virtue? It is, simply, the truth. The truth shall make us free. And the truth about you and me is that, apart from God, we are nothing. We have nothing. We can do nothing. We have a body, but we cannot control it. We do not know when it will die. We have a mind, but the bursting of a tiny blood vessel will make us imbeciles forever. We have a heart that can love, but at times we have no control over it; it is hard and cold and unresponsive to the needs of others. But there is a positive side about this, which was beautifully described by Fr. Faber, Frederick William Faber, the English poet who became a Catholic after Cardinal Newman. He said, "There are some thoughts, which however old they are, are always new, either because they are so broad that we never thoroughly learn them or because they are so intensely practical that their interest is always absorbing. And such thoughts are, for the most part, very common thoughts. They require no peculiar keenness of vision for no one can fail to perceive them. They are like the huge mountains visible to everybody on the plain below." Now, among such thoughts we may reckon that thought, which every child knows, that God loves each one of us with a special love; that God loves each one of you listening to me now with a special love. This is one of the most common thoughts in our religion and yet when we come to look steadily at it, we find it very hard to believe it. God does not look on you in the mass and multitude. As you will stand single and alone before His Judgment Seat one day, so do you stand now. So have you always stood, single and alone before the eye of His boundless love. This is our faith. This is the faith with which you and I must live and die. St. Paul tells us in his Letter to the Philippians, "Let this mind be in you which was in Christ Jesus, Who, although He was God, emptied Himself, taking the form of a servant." Christ divested Himself of His dazzling beauty, of His glory, and He was lost in the crowd and He was thought to be Mary's boy and Joseph's son. And you and I are asked to empty ourselves of all that is false, all that is ignoble, and all that is unreal, so that we may become filled with Christ. Because nature abhors a vacuum, so does grace. I must be filled with something. Tragically, we are filled with all kinds of desires. We want to be applauded. We want to be promoted. We want to be consulted. We want to be loved. We want to be preferred to others. And look at all the fears that fill us, that stifle us and paralyze us. I am afraid of sickness. I am afraid of growing old. I am afraid of death. And I am scared at the thought of what comes after death. Don't you remember Shakespeare, "To sleep, perchance to dream...

what dreams may come when we have shuffled off this mortal coil must give us pause, that undiscovered land from whose bourn no traveller returns...makes us rather bear those ills we have than fly to others we know not of. Thus, conscience doth make cowards of us all." John the Baptist gave us our ideal. "I must decrease, He must increase." All the foolishness, all the unreality, all the intolerance, all the selfishness, all the sin that is in me must decrease so that I can fill the vacuum with Our Lord Who wants to share my life. He wants to be part of the trivia that makes up your waking hours. Whatever happens to you happens to Him. And He wants you to let Him share in it because only then will you find the rest that you crave. A long time ago, St. Francis cried out, "Love is not loved; He comes to His own even today and His own receive Him not." And so, we live lives that are restless and confused and frustrated and unfulfilled because we do not share our lonely life with Him. And so the prayer we learned as children, the prayer that is said all over the world among Christians, is surely our prayer now: "Oh Jesus, meek and humble of heart, make our hearts like unto Thine."

Without Christ

In the Sixth Chapter of St. John's Gospel, we have the immortal words of the Blessed Eucharist. "He who comes to me will never hunger; he who believes in me will never thirst. I AM the Bread of Life. He who eats My Flesh and drinks My Blood has eternal life and I will raise him up on the last day. Unless you eat the Flesh of the Son of Man and drink His Blood, you shall not have life in you. He who eats My Flesh and drinks My Blood, lives in me and I in him. My Flesh is Real Food; My Blood is Real Drink..." These are extraordinary words. And yet, we read in that same Sixth Chapter that many of the disciples could not accept those hard sayings and walked away and no longer walked with Him. I wonder how they lived. Did they live fulfilled, happy lives on this earth? Did they miss Him? Could you and I live fulfilled, happy, successful lives without Jesus Christ? Could people make money without Him? Of course! We are not told that Our Lord acquired anything. But the Gospel tells us He did have one friend who was wealthy, Joseph of Arimathea. Many of His followers gave up everything to follow Him. St. Francis is known all over the world as "the poor man of Assisi who was following the poor Christ." Yes, people can make money and be successful without Christ in a worldly sense. And they can become socially very successful. They can know the right people and go to the right parties without Our Lord. But, my dear friends, surely there is more to life than this. There is another dimension that is deeper and more challenging and more demanding. When Our Lord said to St. Peter, "Will you, too, go away?" he said, "Lord, to whom shall we go? You have the words of eternal life." And it is clear that the effect Christ had on Peter and the other Apostles was profound and lasting. He gave a new meaning to living that they could never forget. He gave them new standards by which to judge themselves and others. And they were so aware of it. If you and I decide to leave Our Lord and to live our lives without Him, we have to ask ourselves, first of all, where will we go for our ideals? The Lord gave us truth, which we can never forget. What would we do without the Golden Rule or the Sermon on the Mount or the story of the Good Samaritan? This is a rule by which you and I can live. When you and I think of truth, we think of Him. When we think of validity, we think of something He said or something He did. Unconsciously, the Lord is part of our lives in ways we do not realize. And it would be very difficult for you and me to walk away and live without Him, because we would leave those ideals behind. And what would we do with the reality of our sin, because for all of us there is the sense of moral failure. Oh, I know we try to forget it and sometimes we joke about it and sometimes we philosophize about it. But in the darkness and the loneliness of a sleepless night, you and I are surely haunted by the fact that we have failed, that we have hurt someone or defrauded someone or neglected someone or ignored someone. If we ever come to the state where we can face this and not be affected by it, we are indeed in deep spiritual trouble. The glory of the Church is that Christ takes our sins away in the Church. You and I in the confessional can hear the loveliest words this side of paradise, "I absolve you from your sins." Our Lord takes our sins and He plunges them into the lake, which is a bottomless abyss of His mercy. And outside that lake there is a sign, "No fishing." Our sins are taken away forever. And if we walk away from Christ and try to live without Him, what will we do with our death? How can we face the end of our journey here in this valley of tears? All our lives are unfinished symphonies. There are still so many melodies that have not been played. There are still so many songs that have not been sung. But He said, "He who believes in me has eternal life." For us, death is not the end. Life is changed, not ended. We are introduced into the fullness of radiant life with the Lord. And so, we can look forward to living and loving forever. And because of Him, we can face more easily the death of our friends and our loved ones. And we can face our own death because of our elder Brother. And so, as we say every day, we say now from our heart, "Pray for us, O Holy Mother of God, now and at the hour of our death."

The Mother of God

Our Lady is "our life, our sweetness and our hope." Some of you may recall the name of an Irish priest who wrote novels in the yesteryears, novels that were very popular, *Under the Cedars* and *Stars, My New Curate*. His name was Canon Sheehan and he was the parish priest of Doneraile, in County Cork. Preaching on Our Lady, he said, "It was decreed by God at the fall of our first parents that, as their children would have inherited grace and glory if His commands had been obeyed, so because of their disobedience their children were to inherit only sin and shame. This law is universal. Not the greatest saints were exempt from it." Once and once only did God create a soul as pure and beautiful at the moment of its conception as it is now in Heaven, a soul to which the Almighty could turn when weary of the deformity which sin had stamped upon mankind. It was the time when the fullness of years had come and it was decreed that the Son should leave the bosom of the Father and take flesh among men. For centuries, God had not created a soul in grace. Yes, he had fashioned and formed them and sent them into the world, but they were in the power of the enemy before they left His Almighty Hands. But now, for an instant, the old time was to come back again, when God could look upon His work and say that it was good and that it did not repent Him that He made it. And so, the Blessed Trinity fashioned and formed and sent into the world the soul of Mary. And God admired His handiwork and the angels bowed down and adored their Queen. And hell, hell trembled at the conception of a Woman who was destined to break the power of its prince. When the Angel Gabriel left the throne of God and came to Nazareth to ask Mary to be the Mother of God's Son, he bowed down before her – so dazzlingly beautiful was she.

Remember, she was God's masterpiece. This is the Girl chosen from all women to give God the color of His eyes, and of His hair. She was to teach the Word to speak in Her own accent. She was to help the Almighty walk His first baby steps. She was to give Him the body and blood in which He would live and suffer and die to redeem us all. The Body and Blood that you and I receive in Holy Communion come from Our Lady. What can we say about her? Words cannot magnify her whom our thoughts can hardly reach. Our praise of Mary, like our praise of God, is best embodied in our wonder and in our love. She was called "Mary," the famous name in Jewish history, Miriam. Miriam was the sister of Moses and in God's inscrutable, providential plan, Miriam helped Moses, the lawgiver, grow. In the New Testament, the new Miriam, Mary, is going to help the Redeemer of the world to grow, to help to save us all. Our Lady is called "Blessed." As She herself said, "All generations will call me blessed." Why? Do you remember the scene in the Gospel when Our Lord was preaching to the crowds and they were hanging on His words because no man had ever spoken as He spoke? And a woman there, knowing she was in the presence of Greatness, not realizing who He was, could not contain herself and she cried out, "Oh, blessed is the womb that bore You." And He said, "Rather, blessed are they who hear the Word of God and keep it." And that is precisely what Mary of Nazareth did. She pondered His word in her heart. She accepted His way with Her, though She did not understand it. So different from you and me. We want to understand. We want to comprehend. We want to be on top of everything. But She accepted God's mysterious ways with her because She knew what you and I say we know – that He loved Her. She believed God loved her. So must you believe it, you whoever

41

you are, and so must I believe it: that we are loved by God with an unfailing, unchanging, and eternal love. We ask Our Lady to pray for us because we are sinners, small-minded people in love with our sins, unwilling to give up our sins, not realizing that the way to peace is God's way, not our own way. And we ask Her to pray for us at the two greatest moments in our lives: this moment and the last. Now is all I have. The next moment is a gift of God to me. As I am standing here now, I must try to be aware of Him Who lives in me, and at the last moment. We must make sure that She is with us then. That is a contract of long-standing, whether She is there visibly or not, that She be there – because then we shall lose all our self-sufficiency, all our sophistication, as we go back to the God from whom we came. If Our Lord had His Mother with Him when He was dying, surely we must make sure that She is with us when we are dying. And so, in the words of the Church, we say, "Pray for us, O Holy Mother of God, that we, all of us, and all whom we love, may be made worthy of the promises of Christ, Your Son and our Elder Brother."

Gratitude

In the Seventeenth Chapter of St. Luke's Gospel, we have the incident of Our Lord's curing the ten lepers. To be a leper in the first century Middle East was not only to be physically sick but also to be socially outcast. The leper could not go to school, could not go to work, could not go to the synagogue, could not go to the marketplace, could not go and associate with others. Because of the nature of the disease, there was the fear of contagion. And so, in their loneliness, lepers banded together for comfort, for inspiration. And ten of them were on the road when Our Lord encountered them. They had to go and show themselves to the priest, because the priest was the one to assure the congregation that they were cured. On their way to the priest from having seen Our Lord, they were cured. One of them, a Samaritan, came back and threw himself at Our Lord's feet to thank Him. And then Christ said, "Were not ten made whole? Where are the other nine?" Was He addressing the leper or the disciples or was He speaking to you and me? Our Lord did not need their gratitude, but He was sorry for them because they needed to give gratitude. James Farley, the once Postmaster General, that wonderful human being, wrote an article that he entitled, *Two Little Words*. He describes a letter he got from a student asking for his help. He went to great trouble to help him. He did much reading and research and sent the results to the student, but he never acknowledged it. And Jim Farley felt so sorry for the student because he did not know how to use two little words, "Thank you." It is so important for you and me that we learn to be grateful because if we are not, it is so easy to become bitter. We imagine that life owes us a living. We imagine we are defrauded. You can understand how the lepers could say, "Why me? Why did this happen to me?" It happens to us that we get what we do not want and our prayers are not answered. I sometimes think of the plight of a young teenager who is angry because he is not allowed to use the family car. Now, He is not making the payments on the car. He does not carry the insurance. He is not liable in case of an accident. And probably, he doesn't buy the gasoline. And yet, he feels slighted. He feels that his rights have not been taken care of. Are we like that sometimes? Are we unreal and selfish and demanding because we are immature? Maybe the problem is not with life, but with us in the deep recesses of our hearts. And then, if you and I are not grateful, there is the danger that we become arrogant. "Oh, I have succeeded." "I am a self-made man." "I have accomplished everything I set my heart on." So, I am not bitter, but I am arrogant and self-satisfied and proud. The tragedy is that this is not true, because we are none of us self-sufficient. We are all of us dependent on others. No one in life has succeeded without having been helped by other human beings. Anything we have, others helped us to get. And, most of all, we are totally dependent on God, Who drew us out of nothingness in the yesteryears; who gives us our next breath and the next beat of our heart. Everything we have is a gift of God to us and we ought to learn to be grateful. For sixteen hundred years, the Church has been thanking God in a famous hymn, *Te Deum Laudamus, Te Dominum Confitemur*. We do not know who wrote it, but eleven hundred years before the Pilgrims ever came to Plymouth Rock, one thousand years before Luther ever penned his protestations on the cathedral door of Wittenberg, nine hundred years before Columbus ever saw the New World, five hundred years before the First Crusade, Christian men and women were thanking God as they heartily sang, *Te Deum Laudamus*. You and I must learn to have hearts of gratitude, to be grateful to Our God with whom we are going to spend our eternity. And so with the poet on this lovely morning, we say, "Oh Lord, You who have given me so much, give me one more thing, a grateful heart."

Suffering

As you know, there has been much discussion in the media of late about the merits of capital punishment – whether it is moral, whether it is wise, whether it is even practical. But in all the animated arguments, pro and con, no one has ever faintly suggested that we have a symbol either of the electric chair or the guillotine. In the time of Our Lord, capital punishment was crucifixion on a cross. It was a symbol of shame and ignominy and failure. And yet, we Christians have made the cross the symbol of our life and of our dreams. As Cardinal Newman said, "It is the cross of Our Dear Savior which has set a due value upon all the hopes, all the rivalries, all the achievements of mortal man." He said, "It is the melody into which all the strains of this world's music are ultimately to be resolved." But what is this thing called "the cross" that you and I hear so much about in our Catholic lives? Is it some sort of otherworld attraction which makes us stand for hours in ice-cold water like the ancient monks, eat a meal now and then and refuse to associate with the crowd? Is that the cross? Ah, no, my dear friends! The cross is nothing else but the anguish of mind, the desolation of spirit, the difficulty that you and I and every child of Adam has in going against himself and trying to live with Our Lord and trying to accept the slings and arrows of outrageous fortune "with Him, through Him and in Him." How do you make a cross? Put down a capital "I" on paper and cross it out. Anything that goes against my selfishness, my sordidness, my imperious nature, my autocratic attitude, so that Christ can come alive in me – this is my cross. My dear friends, we are here in the depth of breathtaking mystery, the mystery of God's love for each one of us "poor banished children of Eve." Remember God created a Garden of Eden where there was neither sorrow, nor tears, nor death. And man, in his selfishness, turned it into a valley of tears. And into the mess that man had made, God Himself came down and lived here, tasting every pain of mind, of soul, of spirit, of body that you and I will ever know. And He is in us now to enable us to accept whatever comes through His permission. But, my dear friends, we must remember that Our Lord's sufferings did not begin on the climb to Calvary. The saddest of the Stations of the Cross is the Eighth Station: the women of Jerusalem mourning for a broken body. They couldn't see His broken heart; and, even if they could, they could never have understood how Love was dying for His own who couldn't care less, for generations yet unborn who would live as if He had never come to save them. Remember Our Lord's sufferings, like yours and mine, came from people. When Our Lord was a baby, they tried to murder Him. He had to become a fugitive, a displaced person. He had to flee from the wrath and anger of Herod. Christ was never fully understood by any human being on this earth. And you know the pain of not being understood by our own families, by our flesh and blood, and by our friends. Our Lord had no support from those in authority; all He had was heckling and condemnation. His words were twisted, taken out of context, given a meaning He never intended. He was falsely reported and the reports were believed. Isn't this the fate of millions in our world today who are lied about through ambition, who are misrepresented, who are misunderstood? Our Lord knew all of this. He tasted this pain in love for us who would have to suffer and endure it now. A man He most trusted, a man who shared the secrets of His heart, a man who ate out of the same plate and drank out of the same cup, betrayed Our Lord. He was betrayed by a kiss of friendship and sold for thirty pieces of silver. Isn't this the fate of millions? But, my dear friends, look at all the ways of suffering in the world. And I would remind you; there is no virtue in suffering. Sorrow never made a saint; tears never brought anyone close to the Lord. The result of these things is to crush a person into tiny pieces and make them sour and cynical and sad and rebellious. Two men were dying with Christ on their crosses, the same self-agonizing death. One of those men turned to Christ in his suffering and he became a canonized saint even before he died, and the other man suffered and died alone. The question you must ask yourself, you who are listening to me – what do you do with the suffering in your life? Are you suffering alone or are you allowing Christ to come into your suffering, teaching you how to grow and develop and become sensitive and mellow and compassionate and real? Because you can leave the Church tomorrow and turn your back on God, but you cannot escape suffering. What you do with your suffering depends on you. He wants to be part of it because He has the secret of radiant living for all of us. Surely the prayer of St. Francis is our prayer, too. "We adore You, O Christ, and we bless you; because by Your Holy Cross you have redeemed the world."

Duty

In the Tenth Chapter of St. John's Gospel, Our Lord draws a comparison between two shepherds. One He calls the "hired hand" and the other the "Good Shepherd." Now, there is no indication that the hired hand was a bad shepherd. He was employed to take care of the sheep, to provide water. The moment of crisis would occur away out in the desert when the sheep were attacked and the hired hand would abandon the sheep. Now, all the money in the world, all the laws in the land could not compel any man to give his life for the sheep. Our Lord tells us He is the Good Shepherd, willing to lay down His life for the sheep. Remember, the Good Shepherd knew each sheep by name. He loved the sheep and would die for the sheep. When Our Lord went to Calvary, He was going way beyond the call of duty. No one could compel or coerce any man to give his life for others. But Our Lord made it clear that no one was taking His life away from Him. Freely He was laying it down as a sacrifice of love to the Father for you and for me. I wonder if we, in our lives, have learned that lesson? There are certain demands, certain duties imposed on everyone on this earth. The employee has to go to work every morning, spend a certain number of hours on the job, and perform certain duties. This is expected. It is the same with a mother and father. They must feed and clothe their children. They must educate them. They must treat them humanely. And so it is with a husband and wife. Certain obligations are laid on them by the fact that they are now one in two and two in one. It is the same with the priest, with the lawyer, with the doctor, with the student. There is another dimension to life that we have to learn if we are going to live radiantly on this earth. The student will never learn the meaning of education until he goes to the library himself, beyond what is demanded of him by the professor, and studies and does research on his own. Then he will begin to enjoy learning for itself. The mother and father and the children will never become a family as such until they go beyond what the law demands. And the man who works will never enjoy his occupation until he stops thinking about the paycheck. Now, my dear friends, in every country, in every community, there are three kinds of people. The lawless who break the law, who refuse to do their duty. They have to be taken care of with the penal system. Then there is the man and woman. They are the people who do what the law demands every day. They are the salt of the earth. And then there are the volunteers, those who go beyond the call of duty. They are the backbone of every country, of every community. But isn't this what Christianity is all about? Isn't that what Our Lord has taught us? To give our cloak as well as our coat, to go the extra mile, not to turn away from him who would borrow from us, to forgive not seven times but seventy times seven times that person, that same person, who does the same stupid things all the time, who is indifferent and callous, who never says, "Thank you," who takes you for granted. Our Lord said, "If you love those who love you, what is there to that? The pagans do that." You and I must love our enemies. We must do good to those who hate us. We must pray for those who persecute and calumniate us that we may be the child of Our Father in heaven, Who causes the rain to fall on the good and the bad and the sun to shine on the just and the unjust. But I need not tell you, my dear friends, because you have been tutored by the years the same as I, that all of this loveliness is not of our own making. This comes only from our union with the God Who lives within us. Without God, we cannot be truly loving to our enemies, truly forgiving to those who hurt us. We cannot be truly understanding and compassionate on our own. This is a gift of God to us. And it comes from the union with Our Lord, which we try to live day after day. Who compels Mother Teresa to do the things she does? Who compels the mother and the father to sacrifice, to do without, so that their children can be educated and grow up and take their places in life? All of this comes from the Lord in whom we believe, who lives within us. So, day after monotonous day, you and I must go on striving, failing, falling, and beginning again. The Lord doesn't ask you or me to succeed in anything. Success is His gift. What you and I are asked to do is to try and go on trying all the days of our life. And so we pray, "Lord, lift me out of my lethargy, my apathy, my coldness, my indifference, and make me so aware of your love for me that I may learn to love you in return."

Sin

I am sure there are very few people in life who aren't touched by the
sight of sadness, and the world is full of sadness. We see it around
us every day – failed lives, broken hearts, shattered dreams. To me,
one of the saddest sights in the world is a rummage sale – a sale
in which almost every item is part of some man, woman or child,
some home, some family, some long-gone holiday of the past, being
sold there coldly, publicly, impersonally; sometimes being sold for
charity, but being sold and given to a stranger. You know the items.
There is the carriage hanging sideways on a broken spring. The baby
who saw the world for the first time from the side of that carriage is
now a man and he has gone out to learn the hard lessons the world
has to teach him. There in the corner is the rug. It seems to be
waiting for the sound of feet that are long since in the grave. There
is the mirror, standing stark and forlorn, before which perhaps a girl
prepared for the one transfiguring moment of her life at the altar or
a woman watched her hair grow grey and saw the inevitable lines
appear under the eyes that had lost their laugh. There is the lamp,
the lamp that lit a thousand scenes of joy and sadness; that burned
far into the night while a student read or a mother waited. There
it is now, homeless and out of place. You can fill in the details for
yourself, but the merciful part is that the lovers of these things are
never there to see strange hands take hold of them. That would be
cruel pain, an agony that's more than human nature could endure.
Yet, on an afternoon of unnatural darkness, a woman had to endure
such pain. Mary had to stand by and see the soldiers come and
claim as their own all that was left of Her Dead Son. There at the
foot of the cross was the little heap of Christ's earthly belongings,
the only heirlooms, the only souvenirs She would have. There was

His seamless tunic that She must have woven stitch by stitch with such love. There was His headdress, which He had mended. There were His sandals, which He had kept clean. And now, these rude, rough men were casting lots as to whose they should be as a reward and recompense for putting Her Son to death. But, my dear friends, we know from our faith that the pain of Our Lady on that afternoon is nothing to what She endures now, every time She sees a soul lose the garment of sanctifying grace; for there, a human being made in the image and likeness of God is brought lower than the beasts – all his beauty is turned into hideousness, all his hope and his love is turned into hatred and despair. There is only one evil in your life and in sin and that is mine. Because sin means we lose Our God. Sin means the life goes out of our souls. Sin means we have become withered branches; fit only to be burned in everlasting fire. We are reminded in the Scriptures that because of one sin, a sin of thought, hell was created. Because of one sin, Adam and Eve were banished from the Garden and all their posterity were cursed, and you and I are living under that curse of God today, which has never been revoked. Because of sin, God once destroyed the world by a deluge. At another time, He rained down fire and brimstone from Heaven. In our lifetime, we've had so many wars and all around us today, there are broken hearts, there is loneliness, there is disease, there is death because of sin. The sinner says, "Away with God! Would that there were no God!" God comes between the sinner and his selfish pursuits. And the sinner has been raising his husky voice and lifting his puny fists in defiance of the creator from the beginning. But that never affected God, not as long as He remained above the clouds. But the moment He came down, the moment He put himself within the sinner's grasp, look at what sinners did to Him. My dear friends, you know that this world of ours is cruel and cold and heartless. But it can be kind. It can be kind to all men on two occasions – at birth and at death; to be born and to die. To come into the world and to go out of it finds hospitality easily, even from the world. How was Our Lord treated on those occasions? Why, it was as much as He could do to get born. It took the Almighty all His time to obtain much acceptance in His own world. He wasn't wanted. There was no room for Him in the inn. Oh, we did hear the angel voices singing His praises on the hillside that night, but those voices are soon changed – changed into the wailings of women, mothers mourning the loss of their sons because man had been seeking God, to murder Him. At his death He wasn't allowed to die a natural death like the rest of men. In the very prime of manhood, life was trampled out of Him as if it were something tiresome and His body was swiftly buried, lest it be polluting the air on the festivity of the city. Have sinners changed? Oh, no. But we want to think about our own sins, our selfishness, our intolerance, our prejudice, our pride, our superficiality, our ingratitude, our indifference to the Lord Who lives within us, Who is longing to share the trivia that make up our waking hours. He has come to us in vain and we must try to remember. I began by talking about the rummage sale. Let me end by talking about the sale of the old violin that was held up and being sold for $2 and $3 until a man came and played a heavenly melody and the people were very moved. "Now the auctioneer said, 'How much am I bid for it? Is it $2000 or $3000? - and going and gone!' said he. But someone shouted, 'What changed its worth? We don't quite understand.' And quick came the reply, 'The touch of a master's hand.' And there's many a soul with a life out of tune, battered and bruised by sin, auctioned cheap to a thoughtless crowd, much like the old violin. A mess of pottage, a glass of wine, a game, and it travels on. It's going once, it's going twice, it's going and it's almost gone when the master comes. And the foolish crowd can never quite understand the worth of a soul and the change that is wrought by the touch of the master's hand."

Greatness

In the Twenty-Third Chapter of St. Matthew, Our Lord contrasts the lifestyle and the behavior of the Scribes and Pharisees with that of His own disciples, telling us how we ought to live. And He says for us, "The greatest among you will be the one who serves; and he who humbles himself, will be exalted." Now, this seems so far removed from our daily living that we forget it. And we don't always understand the revolutionary idea behind it. We think that we are not destined for greatness. Our names will never appear in lights anywhere. But Our Lord is not talking about prominence. That's reserved for the very few. A man can be great without being famous. And a man can be famous without being great. Our Lord is talking about something that is very foundational, something without which no life is really lived. And He's talking about sincerity. I mean, if at the core of one's own being there is dishonesty and deceit, then nothing really matters. Without sincerity we cannot build a life. My dear friends, can you imagine insincerity connected with all the great virtues that we know? Take love. Insincere love. What does it mean? Wouldn't you and I prefer to be hated sincerely than to be loved insincerely? The trouble is that insincerity takes all the lovely virtues and destroys them so that life ends up being a pretense, a game, a make-believe. It isn't whether we are good, but whether we make a good impression. Our Lord said that the Pharisees and the Scribes did their deeds in order to be seen. Now, you and I must understand that there is something of the Scribe and the Pharisee in all of us. There is that hypocrisy in our soul against which we must battle every day. So, we must strive to be honest honestly. We must strive to be real. Our Lord wasn't talking about anything as shallow as fame and fortune. He was talking about greatness, something that we, all of us, want. In our final hours, we want to make sure that our lives are not in vain, that we have counted for something, that our lives have not been wasted. We must honestly try to be sincere in our living, in our dealings with people every day. And then He talked about Humility. Well, we think that's a very accidental virtue. It is nice, but it's not necessary. It's like a picture in a room. It adds to it, but take the picture away and the room remains. And we think of humility as a sort of accessory virtue that is nice to be admired, but not essential. There is a famous man in England whose name is Frank Pakenham. He's known to the world as Lord Longford and he has done so much work for prisoners, for the homeless, for the down and out. He is a convert to Catholicism. Having reached the pinnacle of fame and fortune, he sat down and wrote a book on humility. He discovered that without that, there is not true Christian life. Cardinal Rafael Merry del Val was the Secretary of State to St. Pius X, who was his confidant and his friend. Cardinal Merry del Val's cause has gone forward for beatification. He came on a "Litany of Humility" that was composed by an anonymous monk. And every morning after Mass, Cardinal Merry del Val recited this litany. At the end there is this line, "That others may be preferred to me; Lord, grant me the grace to desire it. That others may be loved more than I; grant me the grace to desire it. That others may become famous and I pass unnoticed; Lord, grant me the grace to desire it.

That others may become holier than I, provided I become as holy as I should; Lord, Grant me the grace to desire it." You see, my dear friends, the challenge is for all of us to become real. It's not that you and I are trying to impress anyone, but to live a life of union with the God Who inhabits the depths of our being; to be aware of Him there; to understand that each one of us has something to do that no one else can do. This is the beginning of greatness. This is the beginning of peace and fulfillment and contentment. This is what our heart desires. And so, with all those who have gone before us, surely we say, "Jesus, meek and humble of heart, make our hearts like unto Thine."

The Agony and the Ecstasy

This lovely hillside and the green fields that surround it remind me of Ireland. In the Third Chapter of the Book of Exodus, we read of the call of Moses. It's fascinating reading. Moses was tending the sheep of his father-in-law, Jethro, and he came to Mt. Horeb. And suddenly he saw a burning bush. The bush was aflame but it was not being consumed. He came near and a voice said to him, "Remove your shoes. This is Holy Ground." And Moses said, "Who are you?" He said, "I am the God of your fathers." And He asked Moses to go to Pharaoh to release His people. And Moses said, "When I go, who shall I say sent me?" He said, "Say I AM sent you. This is my name forever." In the Gospel we find Our Lord saying, I AM the Resurrection and the Life. I AM the light of the world. I AM the good shepherd. I AM the door of the sheepfold. I AM the vine, you are the branches. Live in me so that I can live in you." This is our glory as Christians, that God is living in us in His Son, Jesus Christ, nearer to you and me than we are to ourselves. This is the ecstasy of our religion, that we are other Christs; but the agony is, we do not feel it, we cannot fathom it. We must only believe. Because when you and I were grafted onto the vine, we were given the power to believe Our Lord and what He said, and live out our lives on His word. The great French saint, King Louis IX, built a marvelous chapel, La Sainte Chapelle in Paris, where the Holy Sacrifice of the Mass could be worthily celebrated. And his apartment was next door. One morning his servant rushed in saying, "Sir, come quickly. Christ has appeared on the altar in the Eucharist." And the saint said, "I do not need to see Him there to know He is there. I Believe." "Because you have seen me, Thomas, you have believed. Blessed are they who have not seen and yet have believed." And then, my dear friends, there is the conflict in our soul and in mine with Christ's life and our own. He who is Life has come to us so that we will live His life on this earth, but we are stubborn and we are selfish and we are determined to live our own lives in our own way. We have our own standards. We have our own set of values. And we refuse to let Him take over. And yet, His way is the only way to peace that you and I crave with our whole being. Then we have the agony of trying to remember that He is within us, wanting to share our lives, because you and I forget so easily and we grow weary so quickly. St. Benedict took his monks to choir seven times a day so that they would be reminded of the Lord's living in them. The Muslims are reminded five times a day when they are called to prayer in the Minaret and they worship Allah above the clouds. And the Franciscans remind us three times a day with the *Angelus* when we are reminded of the Good News that the Word was made flesh and dwells among us now in the depth of our being. And you and I, my dear friends, have to cultivate this presence of Our Lord, cultivate it so that we will be changed into Him. In the life of St. Margaret Mary, we find Our Lord appearing to her one morning after Holy Communion and saying, "Margaret Mary, I have given you my heart and now I am taking your heart. And remember from now on, my heart is in you and your heart is in me." But this is what happens to you and me every time we receive Our Lord in Holy Communion. He comes to live in us and we must cultivate that awareness so that we will be changed, unconsciously, but truly into Him; and that we can say with St. Paul, "I live no longer I, Christ lives in me." And surely our dream, our aim is that we can, like the *Man of La Mancha,* bring a measure of grace to our world, that we can become the light in the darkness, that the light shining through us from Him will radiate into the souls around us. When John Henry Newman came into the Church way back in 1845 and became, finally, a Cardinal in the Church, he wrote a prayer that he called *My Prayer.* And I am sure this is the prayer of every one of us this lovely day. "Dear Jesus, help me to spread your fragrance everywhere I go. Flood my soul with Your Spirit and Life. Penetrate and possess my whole being so utterly that all my life may be only a radiance of Thine. Shine through me and be so in me that every soul I come in contact with may feel your presence in my soul. Let them look up and see no longer me, but only Jesus."

Sin of Omission

In the Twenty-Fifth Chapter of St. Matthew's Gospel, Our Lord tells the story of a man who had money and servants and was planning a trip. It is known as the *Parable of the Talents.* Before he went away, he gave one man five talents, to another he gave three talents, and to the third man he gave one talent, and he asked them to trade with these talents until he returned. On his return, the man to whom he had given the five talents came and said, "I made five more." His master said, "Good and faithful servant." The man who had been given three talents did likewise. And the master said to him, "Well done, good and faithful servant." But the one to whom he gave only one talent came forward and said, "I buried your talent because I knew you were a hard man." The master said to him, "You wicked and slothful servant." These are harsh words. Wickedness is not a word that is used very often in the New Testament. Sometimes we call people foolish or crazy or even sinful, but seldom do we call anyone wicked. Why did Our Lord call this man wicked? He wasn't a thief. He didn't steal the money he had. It was given to him honestly. Neither was he a spendthrift. Like the prodigal boy in the Fifteenth Chapter of St. Luke, he could have gone off to a far country with the sizeable amount of money that he had and lived foolishly. He didn't. Neither was he a liar. He could have fabricated some story about the money being stolen, how he had made more money but some thief came and took it all away. No, he wasn't a liar. Then why was he called wicked? Because he did nothing! Our Lord tells the story of Dives and Lazarus. Dives is the rich man and Lazarus sits at the gate every day, the dogs licking his sores. Dives goes to Hades after death, not because he was rich, not because he was immoral, but because he did nothing about the man at his gate. Our Lord tells the story of the man who was going down from Jerusalem to Jericho and was left half dead by robbers. The priest went by and did nothing. The Levite went by and did nothing. They were condemned. It was the Samaritan who came and took care of him. My dear friends, the playboys of the world who do nothing are sometimes put forward to be emulated. But in Our Lord's thinking, this is not so. It is wicked not to work, wicked not to care, wicked not to love, wicked not to pray, wicked not to listen. And then, my dear friends, we are told that the talent he had was taken away from him and given to others. This seems strange at first, but it really isn't. You know, by doing nothing, we can lose so much. Boswell's Dr. Johnson talked about keeping our friendships in repair. You can lose a friendship by doing nothing. Never write to your friend. Never visit your friend. Never answer his phone call. You lose the friendship. A man doesn't have to abuse his wife to lose his marriage. He just ignores her. He never pays her a compliment. He never says "Thank you" for the nice things she does. The marriage dies. A man does not have to bring in salacious literature to destroy his children. He can just ignore them. Show no interest in their school, in their friends. He loses the children. In New York every evening on Channel 5, *The Ten O'clock News* begins, "It is ten o'clock. Do you know where your children are?" And then my dear friends, we find the man condemning himself out of his own mouth, "I knew." Here we are, you and I, we know and we do nothing. We know that Our Lord lives in us. He told us so clearly He wants to share the trivia that make up our waking hours. We never allow Him. We know He lives in those around us. He told us that our final exam would be that we have seen, loved and served Him in those around us, or that we have ignored Him in our neighbor with whom we live. We know all this. We do nothing about it. Sometimes we say we don't even have one talent, we have no talent. This is our self-pity and our immaturity. Everyone can smile. Everyone can listen. Everyone can be kind. Everyone can show an interest in those around. We all have a talent to be used for the glory of God on this earth. We have no excuse if we have faith to do our duty. And so, "We ask Our Lord to teach us to be generous in loving Him, to give and not to count the cost, to fight and not to heed the wound, to toil and not to seek for rest, to labor and to look for no reward except His love."

Our Father

We call it the "Our Father." The great revelation of Jesus Christ was that God is not solitary, that He is Three in One, that Jesus is His Son, and that you and I are called to be His adopted children. Two hundred and forty-five times in the New Testament, the word *Father* is used. God is Our Father. That means that you and I are His child. More than once Our Lord taught us that we have to be converted and become a child before we can enter the Kingdom of Heaven. Francis Thompson, the English poet, wrote a famous essay on Shelley in which he asks, "What is it to be a child?" And he answers, "It is to be something very different from the man of the world. It is to have a spirit yet streaming from the waters of Baptism, to believe in love, to believe in liveliness, to believe in belief. To be so little that the elves can come and whisper in your ears, To see a world in a grain of sand and a Heaven in a Wild Flower, to hold infinity in the palm of your hand and eternity in an hour." You see, a child is full of wonder. A child believes all you tell him. A child snuggles so securely in your arms. A child puts his hand in yours and follows wherever you lead. That is how you and I must be with God, Our Father. And Our Father is in Heaven. Do you ever think about Heaven? St. Paul almost defies us. He says, "Eye has not seen nor ear heard nor the heart of man been able to conceive what things God has prepared for those who love Him." How we need to be reminded, you and I, that we are pilgrims, that we are strangers, that we are wayfarers down in this valley. This is not our home. We have not here a lasting city. We belong to God, and Christ Our Elder Brother has gone to prepare a place for us so that where He is, we may also be. Do you realize as you are listening to me now, with a thousand stray thoughts on your mind, with your worries and your fears and your insecurities, with your plans and your will-o'-the-wisp dreams for a future that you have planned out for yourself that may never come – do you realize that at this moment there is a place in Heaven waiting for you with your name on it? And already today, a thousand times, your guardian angel has passed by and prayed that nothing would so distract you or absorb you or turn your head down here as to make you forget the end for which you were created – to be in that place in glory with the Lord Who loves you. Our Lord said to St. Gertrude, "My Heaven would not be complete without you." This is our faith. What about the Kingdom of God? God's Kingdom is within us and you and I must make sure that the Lord rules over us, not as a president because he goes out of office, but as a King, and that His life and love will penetrate every nook and cranny of our beings, that the Lord will so live in you and me as He desires that we will be able to say with St. Paul, "I live no longer I, but Christ lives in me." And we will live in His Will; His Will on earth as it is in Heaven. Now, what is the will of God in Heaven? Love. There is nothing in Heaven but Love. And God wants everything for you and me on this earth to be filled with Love. And He comes Himself to enable us to accept and to understand and to penetrate the mystery so that we will be able to live lives of love, radiant lives as He intended. Why do we always think that the sad things are God's Will? It's the wonderful things that are God's Will. Dante knew that. "In His Will is our peace." And we ask Him to forgive us as we forgive those around us. These words are very difficult. In effect, I am saying, "Lord, you see my understanding of others, you see my compassion, you see my sensitivity, and you see the way I make allowances? That's the way you must treat me." And sometimes it is so difficult for us that we need Him because we are conscious of our poverty, our inability to cope. And we ask Him to preserve us from evil. The sins we have committed in the past that now come to haunt us, the evil that surrounds us now that beckons to us with the father of lies, promising peace where there is no peace. And the final evil of all that at the end, in our stubbornness, in our stupidity, that we might tear ourselves away from His grasp and choose darkness rather than light for all eternity. We ask Him to preserve us from this, to give something of His won wisdom, that we may understand His love and know that our hearts will be ever restless until they rest in Him. My dear friends, I cannot teach you to pray. No Spiritual Director, no guru, no book can teach you to pray. Only the Holy Spirit, Who is within you, can teach you to say, and to mean, "Abba, Father."

The Love of God

One of the most famous texts in the Scriptures, one especially beloved by the Jewish people, is found in the Book of Deuteronomy. It is called the *Shema*. "Hear, O Israel, the Lord your God is one God. And you shall love the Lord your God with all your heart, with all your soul, with all your mind, with all your strength." This text begins every service in every Jewish Synagogue all over the world. This text is carried about in the pocket of every pious Jew. This text is written over the door of the home of every pious Jew. And every little Jewish boy proudly recites this text on the day of his Bar Mitzvah in Hebrew. "Hear, O Israel, the Lord your God is one God. And you shall love the Lord your God with all your heart, with all your soul, with all your strength, with all your mind." And Our Lord tells us that the Second Commandment is like to the First – that I must love my neighbor as myself. Now, when God tells us to love Him totally, wholeheartedly, that's the way He loves us. In the Forty-Ninth Chapter of the Book of Isaiah, we hear God say, "Should a mother ever forget the child of her womb? Even so, I shall never forget you. See, I have carved your name on the palm of my hand" (Isa. 49:15-16). We sometimes think that is Oriental poetry or rhetoric or hyperbole. Oh, no, it was very real to the people who heard it because in those days, slaves were bought and sold in the public market. And when a slave was bought, the name of his master was carved on the palm of his hand. God is saying, "You are my slave. Your name is carved on the palm of my hand." We don't understand this, you and I. It is too big for our tiny minds. This Love is overwhelming. All we can do is accept it in faith with gratitude. But when God tells us to love Him, He's not asking us to love Him with our own puny, fitful love, but with His own because He has given us His own love. The Holy Spirit has been poured forth into your heart and into mine. And He is the Father's Love for the Son and the Son's love for the Father. And this is the Love I must give back to my God, a Love that is worthy of Him. Love, of course, by definition, has to be given away. The tragedy with us is that we fall in love with God's gifts and forget the Giver. We give our love to mere creatures and we forget that they are God's gifts to us. And we are so in love with His gift of life, we never want to part with it. We want to stay here instead of going back to the Author of Life, the God for whom we were made. And then I must love my neighbor as I love myself. How do I love myself? Oh, I sometimes make mistakes and I do foolish things and I grow weary and I forget.

But I always make allowances for myself. I always come back to reality. I am very resilient. I must treat you in the same way, making allowances for you, for your mistakes, for your foolishness. No, that isn't what He meant. The French say, "*Noblesse oblige.*" Now that I belong to the nobility of God, now that I am a member of God's own family, I must behave in a certain way. I must realize who I am, my dignity as a child of God. I must respect myself and sin must be out of my life. I must respect you for the same reason. You are a child of God, regenerated by the waters of Baptism, the same as I. And the Lord Who lives in me, lives in you. And He tells us in the Twenty-Fifth Chapter of St. Matthew that what we do to those around us, we do to Him. Oh, I know as well as you – I know better than you – that when we look at people through our own eyes, we see their failings, their foolishness, and their sin. But we have been given the faith to go beyond appearances, to dig below the surface and find living there, truly Jesus Christ, the Son of God, Who lives in my neighbor as surely as He lives in me. Sometimes when we have lucid moments, we say things like this, "Oh, God has been so good to me. God has been so gracious to me through the years. God has always bestowed His gifts on me and I am not worthy. I do not deserve it." This is true. Now let me prove my sincerity by showering gifts on those around me who are not worthy by my standards, who do not deserve it, who never say, "Thank you," who take me for granted just as I take my God for granted. Let me try to prove my sincerity by behaving as He does. Surely we pray, "Oh Lord, help me to love you with my whole heart and soul, because otherwise, there will be a lesser love in my life to whom I will be dedicated. I ask you so to teach me how to love you here on earth that I may be worthy to spend my eternity in Heaven where there is only Love."

REFLECTIONS III

Respectable Sins

Did you ever stop to wonder how two brothers in the same family
with the same parents, the same circumstances – could turn out
so differently? One is an excellent student; the other is forever
teetering on the brink of academic failure. One grows up to be a
solid citizen; the other never grows up; he's a perpetual adolescent.
In the Fifteenth Chapter of St. Luke's Gospel, Our Lord tells the
story of two such brothers. One is immature, impetuous, and
irresponsible. He wants his share of the family fortune. He goes
into a foreign country and squanders it all. He comes back broke,
beaten, and badly depressed. The other is quite different. He is
wise, industrious, and dependable. He keeps the rules and stays
home. If he were alive today, he would be a member of the Rotary
Club or perhaps on the Parish Council. When we read the story of
the Prodigal Son, we think of the Prodigal as being the failure in
the family, the black sheep, and the ne'er-do-well; while the elder
brother is the ill-tempered one, the grouch, but not really a sinner. I
doubt if Our Lord would think like that. For Him, the sins of the
Elder Brother were more terrible; not that He belittled in any way
the gross sins of the flesh. They are deadly and destructive. So are

the sins of the spirit, what we call the "respectable sins." They do
not exclude one from polite society, but they are just as common.
When you read the morning paper, you would think the crimes of
lust and violence are taking over the world; whereas we never read
about pride, or selfishness or coldness or indifference, and these sins
are far more common. For every Prodigal out there today, there are
twelve Elder Brothers. For every evil deed that is done, there are a
hundred good deeds that could be done and should be done and are
not done. For every crime of violence, there are a hundred crimes
of indifference. The sins of the spirit are subtler, more difficult to
get at. You know, there is many a Prodigal out there in the world at
this moment, driven there by the haughtiness of the Elder Brother,
because you and I do not have to attack people physically or verbally
to wound them. We can do that with our condescending attitude,
with our superior attitude, with our coldness. Rudyard Kipling, the
English poet of the First World War, wrote a few lines about the two
brothers. "I never was very refined, you see. And it weighs on my
brother's mind, you see. But there's no reproach among swine, you
see, for being a bit of a swine." Driven out by the haughtiness of
others. But one thing the Prodigals of the world have in common –
they know they are sinners. They are aware of their failure and they
feel the need of repentance and forgiveness; while the rest of us, with
our self-sufficiency, we are maybe abominable in the sight of God.
Many years ago, I saw Alec Guinness in a play called *The Cardinal*.
It was probably based on the story of Cardinal Mindszenty. He was
accused of every crime in the book – before he entered the seminary,
while he was in the seminary, as a young priest. He was able to say,
before God, he was not guilty of any of those crimes. Before his
God, he was sinless. And then one day, scrubbing the floor of his

cell in the prison, he was saying the *De Profundis*, "From the depths I cry to You, O Lord," and it suddenly dawned on him that, yes, he was not guilty of those heinous crimes, because he was guilty of a far more terrible crime – the sin of pride. How easy it is for you and me to be blind to the sinfulness that fills our poor souls. Alexander Solzhenitsyn tells the story of his friend, his soulmate with whom he shared his dreams, his ideals. And then, after the war, his friend became a member of the KGB and was guilty of the most heinous crimes. And Alexander Solzhenitsyn asked himself, "How could my friend descend so low?" And he thought, "If I were in the same place, at the same time, under the same circumstances, I too might have joined the KGB and done those horrible deeds." As Dickens said, "There is so much bad in the best of us and so much good in the worst of us that it ill becomes any of us to speak about the rest of us." We are all sinners – the Prodigal and the Elder Brother – and we're all in need of God's forgiveness and God's compassion and God's love. And so, we turn to Our Lady and we say, in the words of the Church, "O Mary, conceived without sin, pray for us sinners in love with our sins; unwilling to give up our sins. Pray for us now and at the hour of our death."

The Building Business

We know that Our Lord was a carpenter. He knew the building business from A to Z. He could have given you and me advice on building a house as surely as advice on building a life. In the Seventh Chapter of St. Matthew's Gospel, at the end of the Sermon on the Mount, He does give such advice. And you and I would do well to hear and heed that advice. He reminds us all that we are in the building business, whether we like it or not. Some are wise builders, some are foolish builders; but whatever our profession, be it butcher, baker, candlestick maker – we are all in the building business. And what we are building is more important than the Eiffel Tower in Paris, or the Golden Gate Bridge in the City by the Bay. We are building a life that will endure when the sun has ceased to shine, when the stars are burnt out, when the Pyramids are returned to dust. And we are each the foreman in our own building. We can choose what to put into the building. Oh, I know we are affected by heredity and by environment, but basically, we are our own masters of our own trade. We know that some take the material and build a cathedral; others take the material and build a shack. Some people from ideal circumstances build a tragic life; others from tragic circumstances build an ideal life. With apologies to William Shakespeare, it is not, "To be, or not to be." We all have to be something. The poet said, "Isn't it strange that princes and kings and clowns that caper in circus rings and simple folk like you and me are builders for eternity? We are each of us given a bag of tools, a shapeless mass and a set of rules, and we each must build 'ere time has flown a stepping stone or a stumbling block." Yes, my dear friends, and the buildings we build are tested, sometimes suddenly, without any warning, like a storm in the desert. Maybe it is a serious illness, the death of a loved one, and the loss of a job, a broken relationship. These things can be tragic. And how we react to them depends on whether we have built our house on rock or on sand. Sometimes the testing is the daily grind. I remember reading once about a man who walked from New York to San Francisco. Arriving at his journey's end, he was met by a barrage of cameras. A reporter asked him, "What was the most difficult thing you had to endure on your journey? Was it the raging rivers or the high mountains, or the weather?" He said, "No, what bothered me most was the sand in my shoes," the daily grind. We have to go to the same job and meet the same people in the same circumstances with the same challenge. You have to work at home, and you have to cook and you have to clean, and you have to begin all over again. You have to go to school, you have to attend classes; you have to write papers; you have to correct examinations. There is no end to it. But He reminded us that our life is lived one day at a time. This evening you and I will leave the world for a while and rehearse for death, in sleep. And at dawn, He will come again to help us face another day. But the challenges, my dear friend, depend on whether we have taken Our Lord's words to heart and built our lives on His teaching. Take His teaching on love. He never varied from that. "Love your neighbor." "Love your enemy." "Do good for those that hate you." "Pray for those that persecute you." "Go the extra mile." "Give your cloak as well as your coat." Love is rock; hatred is sand. Love is strong; hatred is weak. Was He right? You know He was. Nothing was ever built on hatred. You can never build a relationship in your home, in your work, in your community on hatred. Nothing will ever last unless it is built on love. And take His teaching on forgiveness. Forgiveness is rock. Resentment is sand. Forgiveness is strong. Resentment is weak. Ask any doctor about that. The person who ceases to forgive, who harbors resentment, suffers from headaches, insomnia, ulcers, and hypertension. Get rid of the resentment and there is peace and serenity. Learn to forgive. I often think of what a wonderful inner life our Holy Father must live. This man who forgave the one who tried to murder him, and forgave him from his heart. I think of the inner life of Mother Teresa. The peace, the fulfillment she must know, as she realizes that in taking care of the poorest of the poor, day after monotonous day, she is taking care only of Our Lord Himself. This is her privilege; this is her joy; this is her completion. And what about your inner life and mine? Have we built our lives on Him who is the Rock, or do we think we know better? And so, we say, in the words of the ancient prayer, "O Lord, my house is in ruins. You yourself must come repair it to make it a fitting dwelling place for you, and so give glory to the Father through endless ages."

God's Way

In the First Chapter of St. Luke's Gospel, we find God in action, mysteriously, in the first century of our world. His program does not involve any military might or political power. Rather, the meeting of two pregnant women somewhere in Judea. One, Elizabeth, was older. She was to give birth to John the Baptist, the greatest man ever born of woman. The other was young, the most beautiful woman in God's creation, Mary, Our Lady, who was to give birth to Jesus Christ, Our Companion in our exile, Our Savior and Our God. God's ways did not involve any summit meeting in Palestine or Geneva or the convening of any giant corporation. It was just these two women, unknown to the world. The world did not know or could not care what was happening in that Judean place. God works quietly. This is very evident in the Old Testament. We read in the Ninth Chapter of the Third Book of Kings, how Elijah was having one of those days when he was tired of living and scared of dying. He was running away from the wicked queen Jezebel and then God intervened. There was a mighty wind, which loosened the very rocks; but God was not heard in the wind. Then there was an earthquake, which shook everything to its foundations; but God was

not in the earthquake. Then there was a fire, but God was not in the
fire. But finally, there was a gentle breeze and God spoke to Elijah
in the breeze. Have you ever stood in a country lane and watched
the dawn – that irrepressible light that puts the darkness to flight and
then envelops the whole world? There are no trumpet blares; no
banners are unfurled. It is quiet; it is real; it is awesome. In Florida,
in Key West, every evening when the sun sets at the most southerly
point of the continent, people gather there in hushed silence as they
watch the sun descend beyond the horizon. And then, instinctively,
they burst into applause, because this is truly the greatest show on
Earth. My dear friends, you and I are so accustomed to noise and
ballyhoo, we forget that God really speaks to us in the stillness of a
sleepless night, alone before the Blessed Sacrament in the quiet of a
church, or in the secret recesses of our own heart. I am remembering
that on an ordinary day in an ordinary church, an ordinary priest read
the Gospel of St. Matthew and Francis Bernadone was listening,
and his life was changed forever. And God uses small things. In
that first century, everybody thought that what was happening in
Caesar's palace was important. Oh no! It's what was happening in
Mary's womb. I am remembering Europe at the beginning of the
last century. Napoleon was a world power. They trembled at the
sound of his name from the Danube to the Rhine. In 1809, he was so
powerful. We forget the majesty of Napoleon. He dared to kidnap
the Pope! Yes, he made the Holy Father prisoner and compelled
him to crown himself as emperor. In 1809, people were thinking
that what was important in the world was what was happening in
the emperor's palace. No. In 1809, what was happening that was
important was the birth of babies. That year, Abraham Lincoln was
born and William Gladstone and Tennyson and Mendelssohn and a

host of other people. We have long since forgotten the triumphs of Napoleon; but the world, for a long, long time, will be remembering the babies who were born in the year 1809. My dear friends, we are living in an extraordinary era, by God's plan, you and I. And we are witnessing extraordinary miracles before our very eyes. One of them is EWTN. When God wanted to make His self known throughout the world, He did not choose a giant corporation, or some famous cardinals in His Church, or some wonderful preachers. He chose a contemplative nun in her convent, who spent herself and allowed herself to be spent, that the God Whom she worshipped would be known in every corner of the world. And in ways she could not have imagined, none of us could have imagined, Mother Angelica's prayer was heard. And now, EWTN is in the four corners of the globe. May God be praised! But my dear friends, in our own lonely lives, do we sometimes think that when we have grey days and dark nights, that God has forgotten His world and forgotten us? How we need to be reminded again and again, that you and I stand before Our God as if we were the only human beings; that He loves you and me as if there were no one else on earth; and that He died for you and me, and is willing to die ten times all over again rather than we should ever be lost. How we need to hear this. How we need to delve into mystery, which is inexhaustible. How we ask His Spirit of Love to bring it to our minds when we become discouraged and depressed. So, we say to Him on this lovely day, "Oh Lord, Our Father and Our God, help us to understand in a new way that Your love is the great reality in our lives and that your dealings with us, with each one of us, are filled with love. Maybe we will not understand it during our pilgrimage, but we will spend our eternity praising you for the love that enveloped us all our days."

This Is Your Life

Today is a lovely day. The sun is shining in God's world. It is good to be alive. Today is the last day for millions of people all over the world. This is the day written down by God, in love, before they were ever born. Before they ever left His Almighty Hands, this is the day He decided to come take them home. And they don't know it. They all expect to live until tomorrow. People will die today after a long and painful illness, surrounded by their loved ones with great emotion. Some will die alone in a dingy room, men who have been an abysmal failure by the standards of Madison Avenue. The old will die; the young will die; the wise and the foolish will die; the saintly and the sinful. They all expect to live until tomorrow. For you and for me, the last day has been written down, too. Before we ever left God's Hands, He allotted a certain time to me and to you in love; and when that time runs out is His secret, which He will not share with us. He expects us to trust Him. But my dear friends, as today is the last day for thousands and thousands, it is also the first day. All over the world today, children will be born, in your neighborhood, in mine, overseas, in the five continents. Can you go back in imagination to the morning of the day that you were born? The University of Chicago came up with some facts and they are amazing. Can you imagine yourself above the clouds with all the other unborn babies, waiting to be parachuted down to Earth, and you would say to the one next to you, "Where are you going?" And they would say to you, "Where are you going?" And neither of you knew. There's only one chance in twenty that you will be born in the United States. You have the same chance of being born in Soviet Russia. You will probably be born into a non-Christian family – Confucian, Buddhist, and Muslim. If you are born in India, you have only a one in four chance of living more than a year, and if you do survive babyhood, the chances are overwhelming that you will be sick all your life from intestinal parasites, tuberculosis, malaria, or leprosy. This is the fate of most of the children who were born the day you and I were born. Why have we been so favored, so spoiled by the Lord? I don't know. It's a great mystery, the answer to which we will discover only in Heaven. But this I do know – "To those to whom much has been given, much will be required." And much has been given to you and to me that so often, we take for granted. We are reminded that life is God's gift to us; what we do with life is our gift to God. And psychologists today are reminding us that we are like the iceberg. Only one-eighth of us are visible; seven-eighths of us are below the surface. My smiling morning face, my cheery "Hello," and my "Have a nice day" is the one-eighth. The seven-eighths is below the surface where you and I live, where no one sees; where you suffer, where you are hurt, where you dream, where you plan, where you love, where you sin. No one sees that inner life, only God. And you cannot share it with anyone, because they each have their own burden to carry. And you must endure it alone. What do we do with it, you and I? Oh, my dear friends, this is the glory of our religion; that you and I come to Mass, where we are joined to the Lord; who is going to the Father; who is taking you and I with Him. Our Lord came down here. He knows about the seven-eighths. He knows about pain and suffering and loneliness and betrayal and misunderstanding in ways that you and I will have never known. There is no pain of mind, of soul, of spirit, of body that you and I will ever experience that He has not already experienced. And He's in us now, to give us the strength and the staying power we need. And at Mass, we bring ourselves as we are to Him. He takes us and

changes us into Himself, making of your offering and mine a thing
of infinite beauty, because He's God. He can do everything. And
He's madly in love with you. My dear friends, being at Mass is the
most difficult time of the day because it means I must be there in
faith, curbing my wandering mind, realizing where I am and what I
am doing, offering myself to My God, through Jesus Christ, His Son,
My Elder Brother. You and I go to Mass, not to get something out of
it, but to put something into it - ourselves. And then, when we have
made our offering, mystery of mysteries, He comes to live in us, to
share our loneliness and the trivia of the passing hour, to give us the
strength we need to make of our lives something worthwhile. My
dear friend, when you go to Mass tomorrow, or the next time you
go, if you offer yourself as you are to Christ, He will be given great
glory. You will have the peace that He alone can give. You listening
to me and I speaking to you this day will not have been in vain.

Missed Opportunities

In the Thirteenth Chapter of St. Luke's Gospel, we find Our Lord
going to Jerusalem, passing through the towns and villages for the
last time. It was the last time for the people to see with their own
eyes the Fairest of the Sons of Men and to hear with their own
ears the Word of God preached. But then, as now, they were not
interested. When someone asked Our Lord, "Will many be saved?"
and He told about the door being closed and people being excluded,
and they will say, "Lord, You preached in our midst and we ate and
drank with You." And He will say, "I know you not." This is the
story of missed opportunities. Opportunities in life, generally, are
unequally distributed. In Grey's *Elegy in a Country Churchyard*,
Thomas Grey, looking at the graves of so many people who died in

poverty, wrote these famous lines. "Chill penury froze the genial current of their soul." But Our Lord is not talking about those opportunities. He is talking about the spiritual opportunities that every one of us, as a child of God, has on this earth. Every one of us, we are children of God. God has given us His Own Spirit to live in us, and we can all of us bloom where we are planted. But we miss our opportunities, just as they did in the days of Our Lord. America's greatest play, Thornton Wilder's *Our Town*, the mythical town of Grover's Corners in New Hampshire, where people lived and loved and married, prayed, worked and died. In the play, Emily marries her high-school sweetheart and she dies in childbearing. From a place beyond the grave, she wants to go back and relive some of her life. Those in the cemetery pleaded with her not to do it. But she got permission to come back for one day. She chose the loveliest day she could remember, her twelfth birthday. She saw her mother come and wake her in the morning and wish her a happy birthday. She saw her brothers and sisters at the breakfast table wish her a happy birthday. She saw her father, going to work, wish her a happy birthday. She saw the children in school, the party after school, the gifts, the laughter, and the music, the dancing. She said to the Stage Manager, "Oh, it was all so beautiful. Does anyone ever take time to notice?" He said, "Yes, some do, poets and saints." Do you and I take time to notice God's goodness every day in our lives? I was reading recently about a woman, who said that when she was in high school, she was dying to graduate; and how later she was dying to go to college; dying to meet her husband; dying to have children; dying to retire. Now, she was dying, and she had never lived! How easy it is for you and for me to miss opportunities every day. My dear friends, there are three things you can do and must do every day as a child of Your Father in Heaven. First, you can love! God gives you and me His Own Love. And love, by definition, must be given away. You can't keep love. You can't buy it; you can't barter it; you can't sell it; you can't store it. You can only give it away. "A song is not a song until it is sung. A bell is not a bell until it is rung. And love is not love until it is given away to you." God gives us His Own Love that we will give back to His children around us, the human beings with whom we live. Second, you can laugh. A gloomy Christian is a contradiction. You and I have been redeemed by the Precious Blood of Our Lord. We are heirs to the kingdom of Heaven. And we must help those around us to lighten the burden. Because it's a steep climb for all of us and we need all the help we can get, one from another, and laughter lightens the burden. The third thing we can do every day is to listen. First of all, you must listen to the still, small voice within you, telling you that you are not alone, that He loves you, that His strength is with you. And you must listen to the human beings around you. All we need sometimes is a listening ear. You are busy and the phone rings and you say, "Oh, this is Aunt Mary. She'll be on for an hour." That's a holy hour – to listen lovingly, sympathetically, to a human being, because for them, it is therapeutic to talk when you listen. My dear friends, I often think of Mother Teresa. I admire her inner life, her security, her serenity, her certainty, her faith. She knew exactly what she was doing and why she was doing it. She used the opportunities God placed in her life every day. I often think also of Pope John Paul II. I admire how he spent himself and allowed himself to be spent, so that Christ may be known and loved all over the world. In spite of his infirmity, he went without counting the cost to the ends of the Earth. He availed himself of his opportunities. I pray that these words will echo in your heart this day. "I shall pass this way but once. Any good I can do, any kindness I can show, let me not defer it, let me not neglect it. Let me do it now, because I shall not pass this way again."

Firsthand Faith

In the Fourth Chapter of St. John's Gospel, we have the well-known episode of the Samaritan woman. Our Lord goes and sits by Jacob's Well and meets this woman and He asks her for water. They begin to talk. He tells her everything. She said, "I know the Messiah is going to come." He said, "I who am speaking to you am He." She tells the neighbors about Him and they begin to believe her. Then they ask Our Lord and He stays two days with them. And finally, they say they believe in Him, not on her word, but they themselves discover that He is the Savior of the world. My dear friends, our faith must be firsthand. Of course, it starts out secondhand. We have never met Our Lord. We have never touched His garment. We have never been under the secret, supernatural spell that emanated from Him or the divine charm and the loveliness. We know it all from those who lived in His time. Bishop Sheen told me that once he had been interviewed by a reporter who said to him, "Bishop, do you have speechwriters?" The Bishop said, "As a matter of fact, I do." And he said, "Oh, could you ever tell me who they are?" He said, "Certainly! Matthew, Mark, Luke and John." Now, the fact that our faith is secondhand doesn't mean it's second-rate. All knowledge is secondhand – our knowledge of history and geography and science and mathematics. But, it is one thing to know there are great books there; it's another thing to sit down and read them. It's one thing to know about great music; it's another thing to expose my soul to the power of great music so that I am uplifted and inspired. It's one thing to believe in education; it's another thing to go and study and discipline myself in order to become educated. Now, you and I have faith and we must believe all alone. You and I were given the power to accept the Word of Our Lord and live out our days on His Word. He said, "I am the Vine, you are the branches. Live in me so that I can live in you. Unless you eat the flesh of the Son of Man and drink His blood, you shall not have life in you. He who eats my flesh and drinks my blood lives in me and I in Him. And I shall raise him up on the last day." That extraordinary French girl, Thérèse Martin, who was known to the world as the "Little Flower," the greatest saint of modern times, died at the age of twenty-four in her convent in Normandy. She had no ecstasies; she had no visions. She lived by faith alone. This is what she said. "The Lord took me by the hand and led me into an underground passage where there is neither light nor heat. I am willing to spend all my days in this darkness, if only my gloom can bring light to sinners." Faith. She accepted what Our Lord said. She never doubted His Word. Neither must you; neither must I. But faith is hard work. Our Lord was asked by the Apostles in the Seventeenth Chapter of St. Luke to increase their faith. And then He told them what seems like a strange story to us, about a servant out in the fields working hard all day. Our Lord said, "At the end of the day, you don't say to him, 'Come in and dine with me.' Rather you say, 'Come in and prepare my meal.' " Because faith, like work, is constant, it's demanding, it's unglamorous. I have to be coming back to the reality within me all the time, using my faith to discover Him within me every hour because I forget so easily and I grow weary so quickly. And it is surely demanding when there seems no human satisfaction. And it is very unglamorous. No one is cheering us on. No one is applauding us. All alone in the secrecy of our hearts, we must discover the Lord Who lives there and who can be discovered only by faith. St. Paul, writing to Timothy, said that, "Faith makes us strong and loving and wise." Of course that's true. When I know by faith that with Our Lord, who is God is living in me, there is no challenge I cannot face, there is no burden I cannot carry. When I realize that I am never alone, that I'm not lost in the crowd. He loves me with a love for which there are no words. Then I am strong beyond all imagining. Then I am loving, because He has been so good to me. When I look back on my life, in retrospect I see the goodness of God in a thousand ways, proving His love for me. How could I not be loving to others, understanding, and compassionate, making allowances for their weaknesses? The Lord makes allowances for mine all the time. And then I am wise because I understand that nothing really matters, except the Lord. St. Teresa of Avila understood. "Let nothing disturb you, nothing frighten you. All things are passing. God alone is changeless, and he who has God, wants nothing." I am so wise with His Wisdom as I realize that everything passes except Him. St. Francis left a prayer to us, his followers, which we say every day, and I'm sure this prayer finds an echo in your heart now. "O Great and Glorious God, and My Lord Jesus Christ, enlighten, I beseech you, the darkness of my mind. Give me a right faith, a firm hope and a perfect charity. Grant that I may know You, O Lord, so that always and in all things, I may act according to Your Most Holy and Perfect Will."

The Grief of God

In St. Paul's Epistle to the Ephesians, there is the extraordinary sentence, "Do not grieve the Holy Spirit of God." We usually think of making God angry, not making God sad. This says staggering things about God and about us. Do you mean that God makes His happiness depend on you and me? Do we, earthy sinners of the earth, have power over the heart of God? Yes, this is true. What does it mean? It means that God is estranged from those He loves. Heartbreak always presupposes love. Other people can infuriate you, annoy you, disappoint you; but no one can break your heart, except the one you love. Which means that love is a risky business; love makes us vulnerable. And God has taken that risk with you and me. To be estranged from the one you love, to be out of fellowship with them, to be lonely for them, this is an ingredient of sorrow. We don't go far in the Bible to find Our Lord, in Genesis, saying, "Adam, where are you?" Parents experience this sorrow. A mother must teach her child not only to walk, but also to walk away. When children leave home and have other interests and other loves, that is hard. To bring a child to life, to want the best for that child, to pray for it every day, to work hard for it, and then to find the child choose the worst, this is real sorrow. To want fellowship with your child and get only indifference, to want his love and to get only ingratitude, this is heartbreaking. We find God saying in Hosea and Isaiah, "When Israel was a child, I loved him. I took him in my arms... I held him. Now, my people do not know me." We are children of God, you and I, and we are expected to behave in a certain way. The French say, "*Noblesse oblige*. Now that we belong to the nobility, we are obliged to behave in a certain way." And when God gave us His Own Spirit, His Own Secret, His Own Love, there are certain qualities that belong to the Christian soul as a result. St. Paul enumerates them in the Fifth Chapter of Galatians: "Love, joy, peace, patience, kindness, generosity, forbearance, gentleness, faith, courtesy, temperateness and self-control" (Gal. 5:22-23). These are the qualities God Our Father has a right to expect in you and in me. And when He doesn't find them, He is heartbroken. He wept over Jerusalem, thinking of all that might have been. He tells us about the tree that doesn't bear fruit. He tells us about the light that fails and the salt that loses its savor. He's talking about you and me, who disappoint Him. But my dear friends, that is bad enough negatively. When the Lord comes to me looking for love, joy, peace, patience, kindness, generosity, He not only doesn't find those qualities, He finds all the ugliness that fills our souls – pride, covetousness, lust, anger, gluttony, envy and sloth. The seeds of the Seven Deadly Sins are in you and in me. And so often and so easily they predominate in our lives and we become selfish and arrogant and unloving and lazy and moody, totally indifferent to the needs of others, wallowing in our own self-pity or our own self-importance. And when I come to Confession and stammer out my misdeeds, my forgetfulness of the Lord Who lives within me, my indifference to Him in those around me, then I will hear the loveliest words I will ever hear this side of paradise: "I absolve you from your sins," forever. No wonder the Lord says, "What more could I do for you that I have not done?" to remove from our shoulders the burden of our sins. But tragically, we're in love with our sins. I love my narrow mind; I love my intolerance; I love my wagging tongue; I love my prejudices; I love my laziness. I don't want to change! I will give the Lord prayers, but I will not give Him myself. And He wants me – to possess me, to share with me the secret of radiant living, which He has, and to teach me on my journey down here how to love. When we go to Mass, it is Calvary: where we are there in faith; where we offer ourselves to God through Christ Our Brother, who opened the gates of Heaven for us to enter. Listen to the words of consecration! "This is My Blood,

which will be shed for you and for all, so that sins will be forgiven."
This is breathtaking in its beauty. Well, my dear friends, we are poor
sinners. Too often they are our claim to fame; too often we remain
in love with our sins, unwilling to give them up. Turn to Our Lady,
who stood by her Son at the foot of the Cross, and say to Her, with
sincerity, "Holy Mary, Mother of God, pray for us sinners now and
at the hour of our death." She takes us to Him who is the friend of
sinners.

To Know, Love and Serve

Every year, we are graphically reminded of our mortality when,
on Ash Wednesday, ashes are placed on our foreheads and we are
told that our body will return to the dust from which it came. We
are faced with the mystery of life and death. Life is so fleeting, so
uncertain. And we wonder why we are here. What are we doing
on this Earth, you and I? You remember what we learned in our
Catechism – "We are on Earth to know, love, and serve God, and be
happy with Him forever, hereafter." To know God – not just to know
about Him, as we might know about some personage in history or
our best friend – but to know God with an intimacy, a satisfaction,
a completeness, in a way we cannot know any human being. When
you and I were baptized, we were given the breathtaking power
called "Faith," which enables you and me to have a relationship with
Our God, which is the most satisfying experience of our life. And
where is Our God? He is in us, nearer to us than we are to ourselves,
living there in the depths of our being every moment of the day and
night. Our Lord said, "This is eternal life, that they may know You,
O Father, and Him Whom You have sent." And Our Lord, likening
Himself to a shepherd of sheep said, "I know mine and mine know

me." My dear friends, you who are watching me now, there could be
no greater tragedy in your life or in mine than that we should come
to the grave's edge and not know the God with Whom we are going
to spend eternity. St. Augustine prayed, "Lord, that I may know you,
that I may know myself." And to love Him – oh, I'm madly in love
with His gifts. I love life; I love my family; I love my friends; I love
my work. But do I stop at the gifts and miss the Giver? Whoever
you are, listening to me now, remember, however weak or wayward
or wicked you may be, God is madly in love with you, whether or
not you love Him. Why is Our God so foolish? Because His name
and His nature is "Love." In an act of love He drew you out of
nothingness in the yesteryears, and that love has sustained you and
enveloped you every single moment since then. The next breath you
and I draw is an act of God's love for us. Were He to cease to love us
for one instant, we would cease to be. And to serve Him! How easy
it is to put myself at the center of the universe, and I am preoccupied
about my comfort, my happiness, my health, my welfare, and my
work. I am not the center of the universe; God is! And I am here
on this earth for a few fleeting years – seventy or eighty, if we are
strong – in which to serve God. Every morning, God gives you
and me 1,440 minutes in which to serve Him. What do we do with
the time God gives us? How easily we waste it, we squander it. I
wonder how you and I will begin to think of time when the hourglass
is running out and we can see in the faces of those around us that
this is it, that it's all over. Will we talk then about "killing time"?
Will we "find time heavy on our hands"? St. Teresa of Avila, we are
told, took a private vow never to waste a moment of time, because
she knew that the moment that secured Heaven for the Good Thief
would secure it for us, too. And when it's all over and the battle has

been won, what is our destiny? We are told it in the Twenty-Second Chapter of the Book of Revelation, the last of the seventy-two books of the Bible. "Then we shall see Our God face to face. His name will be written on our foreheads. It will never be night again. We will not need lamplight or sunlight, because the Lord God will be shining on us and we shall reign forever and ever" (Rev. 22:4-5). That is your destiny and that is mine. Louise Haskins, an American writer, wrote something that has become very famous. I think you will like her words. "I said to the man who stood at the gate of the year, 'Give me a light that I may tread safely into the unknown.' And he said to me, 'Go into the darkness and put your hand into the hand of God, and He shall be to you better than light, and safer than any known way.' And so I went into the darkness and I found the hand of God, and He led me to the breaking of the day in the East." The poem prayer of Cardinal Newman is known and loved all over the world. John Henry Newman was a very devout Anglican who discovered he was not in the Church that Christ founded. He thought he would go to Rome, and he did. But his problems were not solved in Rome. He was very confused, very restless. He was returning to England on the ship and one night he could not sleep. He got up and he paced the deck under the stars of the Mediterranean, feeling the immensity of God and his own littleness. And he wrote these lines. "Lead, kindly Light, amidst th' encircling gloom; Lead Thou me on! The night is dark, and I am far from home; lead Thou me on. Keep Thou my feet; I do not ask to see the distant scene; one step enough for me. Lead, kindly Light. I was not ever thus, nor prayed that Thou shouldst lead me on. I loved to see and choose my path; but now, Lead Thou me on! Lead, kindly Light."

The Greatest Commandment

In the Twenty-Second Chapter of St. Matthew's Gospel, a lawyer asks Our Lord, "What is the greatest commandment?" (Matt. 22:36). And He answers, "This is the greatest commandment: You shall love the Lord your God with your whole heart, with your whole soul, with all your strength, with all your mind; and you must love your neighbor as yourself" (Matt. 22:38-39). Why should I love God with my whole heart, with my whole soul, and love my neighbor as I love myself? Why should I love myself? Because I am a child of God and God's Son is living in me. There is a play in New York that has been running for thirty-five years, called *The Fantasticks*. It is a play about young, tortuous love. And it begins with the heroine coming on the stage singing, "I am special. I am special." Every one of us can sing that song. Listening to me now, whoever you are, you can say before Your God you are special. He created you especially with something to do on this earth that no one else can do. And you must love yourself because of who you are. One remembers Simon Peter's encounter with Our Lord at the lakeshore. His brother Andrew had brought him to Our Lord, and Our Lord said to him, "You are Simon. You are the rock on which I'm going to build My Church"; Simon - impetuous, arrogant, selfish. From now on, think of the self-image he had – the rock on which Christ was going to build His Church. But his brother Andrew is a famous saint in the Bible. Andrew was the first human being ever to follow Our Lord. He found Him at the lakeshore and he went and he said to his brother Simon, "I have found the Messiah." Immediately Andrew lost the first place. Simon's name was changed to Peter; Andrew's was not. There were two sets of brothers – Peter and Andrew; James and John; and Our Lord broke up the foursome. It was now Peter, James and John. He took them up on the mountain, gave them a vision of Heaven. He took them into the Garden at the end. He left Andrew outside. Did Andrew pout and sulk? Did he have an inferiority complex? No. The Gospel is quite clear, because the day Our Lord wanted to feed the five thousand, no one could think of anything. It was Andrew who found the boy with the five barley loaves and two fishes. And at the end of Our Lord's life, some Greeks came seeking Him. It was Andrew introduced them to Our Lord. You see, Andrew had achieved his life's ambition. He had found the Lord. Have you? Have I? It's a long time since St. Leo cried out, *"Agnosce, O Christianae, dignitatem tuam."* which means "Realize and understand your true dignity, O Christian." You are a child of God. Jesus Christ is living in you. And I must love my neighbor for the same reason that I love My Lord. It is interesting that in the story of the Good Samaritan, everyone in the story is named. There are the robbers, there is the priest, there is the Levite, there is the Samaritan, and then there is the nameless man, the certain man found half-dead on the side of the road. He had no name because it doesn't matter. Love is no respecter of persons. Everyone must be loved because Our Lord is in the people around us. When I think of all the noble women in this country who are taking care of ailing husbands, with no gratitude, with no recompense, with no recognition, simply doing their duty because they promised God at the altar on the day of their wedding that they would love their partner in sickness and in health – they are the unsung heroines. And all the children taking care of aged parents who are difficult and demanding because of their years. And the children are doing this out of a sense of duty and loyalty and love, when there is no emotional satisfaction. This must bring joy to the angels in heaven and gladden the heart of Our Lord. And then you and I must love Our God with total and absolute love in a way we cannot love any creature. Remember, God never had to create you – never. He created you for glory and your place is waiting for you now. And we are told in the Book of Revelation that when God created us, He gave each of us a name known to Him alone. When He utters that name, you and I will recognize it and we will fly back to Him faster than sound, back to the God from whom we came. And when we meet Him, He will not ask you and me, "Why weren't you like St. Francis or the Holy Father or Mother Teresa or the Little Flower?" No. He will say, "Why weren't you like you, that unique creation of mine? That radiant human being I intended to live on this earth, in whom I could shine?" How disappointed we will be when we find that we have disappointed Him. But my dear friends, you must think about death and about heaven. Remember, your destiny is there. You are a pilgrim, a stranger, a wanderer down here in this valley of tears, and your name is on your place in heaven now, at this moment. And a thousand times today, your guardian angel has passed by and seen your name there and prayed God that nothing would so distract you or absorb you down here as to make you forget the end for which you were created – to live in the glory and the joy and the bliss which "eye has not seen, nor ear heard, nor the heart of man been able to conceive." Surely the prayer of St. Ignatius, the great founder of the Jesuits, is our prayer today. "Teach me, My God, to be generous. Teach me to love and serve you as you deserve, to give and not to count the cost, to fight and not to heed the wounds, to toil and not to seek for rest, to labor and to look for no reward except your Love."

The Christ Who Needs Us

All good human relationships are based on human respect, human trust and human need. This is true of husbands and wives, parents and children, employers and employees, friend and friend. And it is true of our relationship with Our Lord. We respect Him and He certainly respects us. He never intrudes. There is no coercion, no compulsion. He allows us to be free. We trust Him. We certainly do. And He trusts us. It is mind-boggling to realize that the Almighty God entrusts Himself to us totally in Holy Communion. We need Him. Oh, and how we need Him! Some of us cannot imagine a day without the Lord. And strange as it may seem, He needs us. Look at His life. He needed Our Lady to be born. When He was growing up, as a teenager, He needed St. Joseph to guide Him. He needed John the Baptist to baptize Him. He needed the woman of Samaria to give Him a drink. He needed the little peasant boy to give Him five barley loaves and two fishes to work the miracle. He needed Peter, James and John to go and stay with Him in the Garden. He needed Simon of Cyrena to help Him carry His cross. He needed Joseph of Arimathea to find a place for Him to be buried. And after His Resurrection, He needed the Apostles to go out and make disciples for the Father's glory. You know how something responds in us when we are needed. Imagine being in bed at night, asleep, when you hear a cry for help, how we respond to the need. I was reading recently about two test pilots. They were sent in two planes to test them and they were above the stratosphere, going at tremendous speeds. And one of them thought his friend was in trouble, as if the oxygen was not working. So, he thought, "My friend is in trouble. How shall I get to him?" And he cried out, "I can't make it!" and immediately, his friend heard that and descended to a lower level. He saved his life. My dear friends, how true it is that the Lord is the Master and we are the servants; He is the Teacher and we are the pupils; He is the strong one, we are the weak ones. But it is also true when the poet wrote, "He has no hands but your hands to do His work today. He has no feet but your feet to lead folks in His ways. He has no lips but your lips to tell them how He died. He has no love but your love to bring them to His side." That has been the inspiration of Christians since He ascended into Heaven. This is the inspiration of the Holy Father as he goes around the world to make Our Lord known and loved by His children. This is the inspiration of Mother Teresa as she spends herself day after day taking care of Him in the poorest of the poor. This is the inspiration of every missionary alone under alien skies, spending themselves for the Lord Who needs them. This is the inspiration of every nun and of every priest who leaves everything to follow Our Lord. When I think of the noble women I have encountered through the years – all my Franciscan sisters, the Sisters of Mercy, the Sisters of St. Joseph – who spend themselves teaching, day after monotonous day, to help young people find their place in life. I think of the Poor Clares and the Carmelites who are incarcerated for love, who get up at midnight to pray for the world that's sleeping and is not interested. I think of the Trappist monks who work and pray, all trying to prove to the Lord that it was not in vain, that He was not a fool. This is the inspiration of every Catholic mother and father, who are trying to rear their children and mold and fashion them in the likeness of Christ. This is the inspiration of every Christian man and woman who goes into the marketplace to try to make the Lord known, to be a witness to Him in the dark places. This must be our inspiration for every day that dawns. Surely the *Prayer of St. Francis* is our prayer.

"Lord, make me an instrument of your peace on this Earth. Where there is darkness, let me bring your light. Where there is despair, let me bring hope in you. Where there is hatred and animosity and confusion, let me bring your love. Let me seek not so much to be consoled as to console; to be understood as to understand; to receive as to give. For it is in giving that we receive." Haven't you been tutored by the years the same as I and discovered that in giving yourself and spending yourself for others you receive a fulfillment, a serenity, a peace that defies description? "And in dying..." Dying to our selfishness. "...That we are born to your eternal life."

The Purpose of Life

When you read the obituary notices in the paper on any given morning, are you surely not reminded of Grey's *Elegy in a Country Churchyard*, "...And know that all the paths to glory lead but to the grave." However long a human being lives, his life, in comparison with eternity, is like a flash of lightning. We are told in Psalm 89 that our span of years is seventy, or eighty if we are strong, so that when we reach the three-score years and ten, after that, we are living on borrowed time. And it is God's plan that you be alive at this time in history, not a hundred years ago, and not a hundred years hence. And your life and mine is ebbing away. And we realize that we are on this Earth for one purpose and we learned that purpose in the Catechism, at our mother's knee. We are here "...to know, love, and serve God and be happy with Him forever hereafter." And to know God – not know about Him, not as one would know about George Washington or St. Augustine, or St. Elizabeth Ann Seton – but to know Him with an intimacy, completeness and satisfaction; in a way that we cannot know any human being. And this is because of the faith that was given to us when we were baptized. Our Lord said, "This is Eternal Life: that they may know You, O Father, and Him Whom You have sent." I read a story of a woman in New York, during the Depression. She was a widow. She had three growing children. She went to work every day to put food on the table. One Friday evening, she came home and she announced that she was giving a party. The children were delighted. "Mom is giving a party! She has been promoted; she has been given a better job." They said, "Mom, why are you giving a party?" She said, "Because I've lost my job." "You've lost your job? And you're giving a party?" "Yes," she said, "I am celebrating in anticipation of what God is going to do for me and you, because I know He loves us." She knew Him. Do you? Do I? The great psychologist Carl Jung, when he was an old man, was asked by a cynic, "Do you still believe in God?" He thought for a moment, and he smiled and said, "I no longer merely believe. I know." My dear friend, could there be any tragedy greater in your life or in mine than that we should come to the grave's edge, on the threshold of eternity, and spend our days with a God whom we have not grown to know? That would be tragic, indeed. And to love Him, how do we love Him? My dear friends, we are so in love with ourselves. We are in love with all the things around us. We love our wives, our husbands, our children, our position, our health, our happiness, and our friends. We love all these things – God's gifts to us. Everything we have, God has given to us. We are so much in love with the gifts, that we have forgotten the Giver. We are so much in life that we don't want to die. We don't want to give up life to go back to the author of Life. How strange for us who say we believe. My dear friends, if there could be any sorrow in Paradise...If there could be any tears in Heaven, your heart and mine will be broken, when we realize how shoddy we have treated the God who has loved us every moment with a love for which there are no words; beyond our imagining. Then, there is our service of Him. How do we serve Our God? Many years ago, I remember a program on television – the name escapes me – but it was, every week, someone was suddenly told they had inherited a million dollars, and the donor wanted to see how they would spend it. Some were very generous with their family, their friends, and with the poor. Some hoarded it and never spent it. Suppose every day you and I were given $1,440 that we had to spend, every day. We could not keep it; we could not put it in the bank. We had to spend it, every day. You and I are given 1,440 minutes every day. Do we spend them for the glory of God or are they wasted and squandered thoughtlessly? You see, how important our "Morning Offering" is, when I offer to God my every thought, word and action this day, for the glory of My Father and My Creator and My Redeemer. I give back to God, in love, all that He has given to me. St. Teresa of Avila took a private vow never to waste a moment of her life. And surely, Psalm 62 is our prayer today. "O God, You are My God. For You I long. For you my soul is thirsting. My body pines for you like a dry, weary land without water, so I gaze on you in the Sanctuary, for Your Love is better than life."

Discipleship

Did you read the interview with the great Russian spy, Sonja? She is thought to be the greatest spy of the century, the modern Mata Hari. She is brilliant. And when she was young, she was very beautiful. She wandered all over the world charming diplomats and got their secrets and returned them back dutifully to the KGB. Now, the KGB is only letters on a printed page. Sonja is an old woman. She has no money; she has no friends. The interviewer asked her what she was going to do now, with the rest of her life. She said, with tears in her eyes, "I don't know where I can go or to whom I can turn." My heart aches for that woman. She gave her life to an ideal, to a dream that turned out to be false. How grateful we ought to be to Our God that we are disciples of Jesus Christ, Who is yesterday and today, and the same forever. He said to the Jews who would be His disciples – we read this in Chapter Eight of St. John's Gospel – "If you would be My disciples, then listen to My Words, for they will lead you to the Truth, and the Truth shall make you free" (John 8:31-32). The whole of religion is listening. God speaks and man listens. God spoke to Abram; Abram listened. He left his home and his father's country and set out for the land God would show him, not knowing where he was going. He listened to God. And Abram was seventy-five years old. God spoke to Moses and asked him to do an impossible task. Moses listened when God said, "I shall be with you." Solomon prayed God for a listening heart. The boy Samuel said, "Speak, Lord, for your servant is listening." Our Lord took the three disciples, Peter, James and John, up on Mt. Tabor, where He was transfigured before them. And the voice of the Father is heard saying, "This is My Beloved Son. Listen to Him." Because you and I listened to Our Lord, we know that God is Our Father. We could never have known this; we could never have imagined it if Christ had not told us. Because we listened to Him, we know that God has numbered the very hairs on our head, that not a sparrow falls to the ground without His knowledge and His permission. Because we listen to Him, we know that we are branches of the vine, that

He is living in us, and we are living in Him. And because we listen to Him, we know that He has gone to prepare a place for us, that where He is, we also may be. But, my dear friends, this listening is not only with our ear, but with our heart, with the "inner ear." If you spell the word "heart", h-e-a-r-t, it has an "inner ear." We must be constantly listening, constantly learning, constantly penetrating, and constantly obeying, because the Word of God is inexhaustible. I read about a new priest who went to the parish and amazed everyone with his prowess in the pulpit. The first Sunday, the people were speechless. The second Sunday, people came to church who hadn't been there for a long time, but he preached exactly the same sermon, word-for-word. On the third Sunday and the fourth Sunday and the fifth Sunday and the sixth Sunday, he preached the very same sermon, word-for-word. Finally, two little old ladies in white sneakers came up to him one day and said, "Father, don't you have any other sermon?" He said, "Yes, I have a hundred other sermons, but I shall do something about the second sermon when you have done something about the first sermon." It isn't only that I listen, I must learn and put it into practice and His words will lead me to the truth. I must discover that Our Lord's Word is true, that His Word works in my life. When David, in Psalm 23, said, "The Lord is My Shepherd," this was a statement of fact born of conviction. "The Lord is My Shepherd; there is nothing I shall want.' " David knew. I read about Charles Laughton as an old man living in Hollywood, being asked to speak at the Communion Breakfast. He regaled people with tales of his work in the movies, and in the theatre, and he ended by saying, "Let me quote my favorite Psalm, Psalm 23. 'The Lord is My Shepherd, there is nothing I shall want.' " In the audience was an old, old priest, a great admirer of Laughton, who was now totally deaf, never heard a word, but was happy to be in the presence of the great actor. The pastor asked him to give the final blessing, and he stood up and he said, "The Lord is My Shepherd; there is nothing I shall want." Someone went to Charles Laughton and apologized and said, "You see, Father didn't hear. He was deaf." And Charles Laughton said, "Ah, I know the Psalm, but he knows the Shepherd." I must prove the Truth and the Truth will set me free. Free from what? All those demons that bedevil us inside – fear of growing old; fear of being sick; fear of dying; and fear of what comes after death. But St. Paul said, "O death, where is your victory? O grave, where is your sting?" And St. Francis said, "Welcome, Sister Death. I have no fear now, because I can do all things in Him Who strengthens me. I have discovered He is living within me, My Lord and My God." And so, the words of the old hymn are surely ours this lovely day. "Alone with none but Thee, My God, I travel on my way. What need I fear when Thou art near, O King of Night and Day?"

REFLECTIONS IV

Radiant Living

The pagan philosopher Frederick Nietzsche was once addressing a group of Christians and he began by saying, "Aren't you supposed to be redeemed or something? You don't look redeemed to me. Aren't you supposed to be radiantly alive? Most of you look half dead." Could this be said of us, too? Our Lord gave the secret of radiant living. He said, "I have come that you may have life and have it more abundantly. I am the Life." In the Sixteenth Chapter of St. Matthew's Gospel, He gives the formula for all who care to listen. "If anyone wishes to come after me, he must deny his very self, take up his cross and follow me. He who would save his life will lose it and anyone who loses his life for my sake will find it." Lord, are you serious? Say that again. "If anyone wishes to come after me, he must deny his very self and take up his cross and follow me. The one who would save his life will lose it and the one who loses his life for my sake will find it" (Matt. 16:24-26). This is a hard saying. But, my dear friends, Our Lord wasn't talking only about religion. He was talking about life. Total dedication is demanded of science, of education, of the arts, of sports. When I was growing

up in Ireland, a long time ago, the legend in the musical world was
Margaret Burke Sheridan. She was a girl from County Mayo. Her
parents had died and she lived with the Dominican Sisters in Eccles
Street in Dublin for her education. She had a very beautiful voice
and won every medal. At the end she won the gold cup. Her father
had a friend who was a Member of Parliament in Westminster and he
took her to London and she lived with Lord and Lady Birkenhead.
I got to know Margaret when she retired. She told me that when
she was a young girl she used to sing for their friends. One night,
she was told a very special person was coming from Italy. She told
me, that at the time she sang in a wretched Italian. But she sang
for the man and friends anyway. When she finished singing the
gentleman grabbed her and said, "What are you doing here? You
have the loveliest sound that God ever gave a human being." This
was Marconi, whose mother came from Wexford. He took her to
Italy and she never came back. She became the darling of La Scala
in Milan, the friend of Puccini and Toscanini and all the great ones
of her day. She said to me that when she sang for the maestro in
Rome, the greatest music teacher, he said to her, "Young lady, have
you come to Italy to sing or to learn how to sing?" She said, "I've
come to learn how to sing." Then he said, "You must become a poor
student and go to live with the other students and learn the meaning
of hardship." And she said to me, "It was then that I understood the
meaning of the nuns' lives in the Dublin orphanage where they raised
me, the hardships they had to go through to serve others. When
I had to sacrifice for my art, it taught me that all men and women
had to do so if they were to find the Lord." But when the Lord said
that I must deny myself and take up my cross, remember we have
many selves. There is my courageous self and my cowardly self.

There is my generous self and my mean self. There is my brave self and my timid self. And we could go on and on. The self Our Lord is talking about that I must lose is my sinful, selfish self; and the Cross, which is what everyone on earth has to endure, the slings and arrows of outrageous fortune. Do I take them up and give them to Him and suffer with Him, or do I stoically suffer alone excluding Him? Dietrich Bonhoeffer was a German theologian who taught in the Theological Union in New York. He was imprisoned for having been discovered involved in a plot to overthrow Hitler. He wrote famous letters from prison. And he said, "When a human being meets Jesus Christ there can be no co-existence. The Lord and I can't live together. He must take over." As St. Paul says, "I live no longer I, It is Christ Who lives in me." And unless I am willing to pay the price – and my dear friend, it isn't as great as it seems – it means that every day, every hour of every day I try to let Him take over. He has given me His Spirit to encourage me, to inspire me, to teach me, to remind me how to do things His way, with graciousness, with understanding, with compassion, with forgiveness, with love, so that I will leave the world a better place than I found it. And so, I pray, "O, Lord, I am weak, I am foolish, I am fearful. I want you to take possession of me really and truly so that you can live in me and shine through me in ways that I will never know. You will be given the glory. That is all that matters."

God's Truth

In the Thirteenth Chapter of St. Matthew's Gospel, Christ speaks to us through the *Parable of the Sower.* It is surely a scene with which He was familiar in His home country. "A Sower went out to sow seed by hand. Some of it fell on the footpath, on the wayside; some of it fell on shallow ground; some of it fell among thorns; and some of it fell on good ground and produced fruit, some a hundredfold, some sixty, some thirty." (Matt. 13:3-8). This is surely the way we react to the Word of God. We are reminded that we do not live on bread alone, but on every Word that proceeds from the mouth of God. And the Word of God falls on hard ground, on the footpath, and it cannot penetrate. Ask any doctor about that – the number of men who have shortness of breath, palpitations, and chest pains. They refuse to go to the doctor, lest they discover the truth. And the women who have signs on their body that they may have cancer refuse to go to the doctor, lest they discover the truth. And the truth for you and me is, we are children of God, here for a few fleeting years; and the day of our exit from this world was already written down before we were ever born, but we refuse to think about it. The devil doesn't try to tempt you and me by saying, "There is no Heaven," or "There is no God," because our instinct tells us there is. But he always gets us by telling us, "There is no hurry. I am young, I am healthy, and the world is at my feet. 'When I am old and grey and full of sleep,' as the poet said, then I'll have time to think about it all. But now, now I am busy with other things." So, the Word of God never penetrates my mind. And then the seed that falls on the shallow ground grows up quickly. But it is withered by the heat of the sun. Some older parents could tell you about that. They once were young. They had children. They knew it was their duty to love them and care for them and spend time with them. But Father had his career and Mother had a job. And suddenly the children are grown and gone. And those lost opportunities never return. My dear friends, we have only today. Yesterday is a word. Tomorrow is a word. All we have is this day that God gave to us, freshly minted from His Hand to you and me, in love. The 17th-century Jesuit Fr. de Caussade coined the felicitous phase, "the sacrament of the present moment." Your life and mine is given to us moment by moment by moment, in love. And I have only the present moment to be aware of who I am. My dear friends, look at all the good resolutions we make after Mass on Sunday. We were inspired by the sermon and we are going to do this or that. But of course, we never do. The story of the minister with his little flock, and he heard that now they were involved in telling lies, in untruths. And on Sunday morning he said to them, "It has been brought to my attention that you tell lies so easily and so often. Now, during the week, will you promise me that you will all read the Seventeenth Chapter of St. Mark and next Sunday, we will discuss it." And they agreed. The next Sunday, he said, "How many of you have read the Seventeenth Chapter of St. Mark?" They all put their hands up. He said, "You're all telling lies. There is no Seventeenth Chapter of St. Mark." My dear friends, our good resolutions are not sufficient. "I am going to do so much in the years to come." What am I doing today? It's all I have. And then, the seed that falls on the ground and grows, but it is finally choked with the thorns – it never gets anywhere. How easily that can happen for you and for me, preoccupied, worried, distracted, caught up in things that do not matter. And the Word of God and our idealism and our growth are stunted, and we never become what God intended we should be. We are near great. And finally, the seed that falls on good ground and brings forth fruit. You say, "But there is so little I can do." Oh, my dear friends, every one of us can love. I can love the human being next to me, who is demanding, who is difficult, who is uncooperative. I must learn to understand, this human being has his own problems, his own secret suffering, his own cross known to him alone. I have never walked in his shoes. I do not know where he is coming from. And I can and I must, by the grace of God, learn to love him today. It is all I have. I came across this little piece of doggerel recently. It rang a bell with me. "Go give to the needy," my angel said, "For giving is living." "Must I keep giving again and again?" my petulant answer rang. "Oh, no," said the angel piercing me through, "only stop giving when God stops giving to you."

The Heart of God

As you know, we are not as familiar with the Scriptures as we ought to be. There are seventy-two books in the Bible, and all of them were written by Jews, except one - St. Luke. He was a Gentile and he was a doctor. He wrote the Gospel that bears his name, and he wrote the Acts of the Apostles, which was a history of the early Church. St. Luke's Gospel is called, "The loveliest book in the world." It's the book of prayer. St. Luke tells us more than the other evangelists about the times Our Lord prayed. He prayed before He chose the Apostles; He prayed on Mt. Tabor; He prayed in the Garden, in His Agony. It is the book of praise. It has the three great canticles that we use in the Divine Office every day - *The Canticle of Zechariah*, the father of St. John the Baptist, the canticle he recited when he had received his speech again. "Blessed be the Lord, the God of Israel" (Luke 1:68). We say that every morning in our morning prayer. St. Luke includes *The Canticle of Our Lady - The Magnificat*. She said that when she went to visit her cousin Elizabeth and Elizabeth said to her, "Whence is this to be that the Mother of My Lord should come to me?" (Luke 1:43) And then Mary said, "My soul magnifies the Lord; my spirit rejoices in God My Savior" (Luke 1:46). And then it has *The Canticle of Simeon*, the old man who was told by the Holy Spirit that he would not die until he had met the Messiah. And when he took the Child in his arms, he said, "Now you may dismiss your servant in peace, O Lord" (Luke 2:29). We say that canticle every evening in our Night Prayer. St. Luke is the Gospel of women. St. Luke tells us about Martha and Mary, about the widow of Naim, about Elizabeth. And St. Luke is the Gospel of the Infancy, telling us about Our Lord's birth and His youth. In the Fifteenth Chapter of St. Luke, we have the incident where the Scribes and Pharisees were gathered together and Our Lord was talking to street people, the publicans and the sinners. And they said aloud, "He eats with publicans and sinners" (Luke 15:2). Then He told three parables – the most inspiring, the most beautiful, the most consoling parables in the world, all contained in the Fifteenth Chapter of St. Luke's Gospel – the stories of the *Lost Sheep*, the *Lost Coin*, the *Lost Boy*. The Scribes and the Pharisees saw only a crowd of publicans and sinners. Our Lord saw individual human beings, and He told them about one shepherd looking for one sheep, one housewife looking for one coin, and one brokenhearted father looking for one lost son. They didn't understand the heart of God. Neither do you and I. It is too mysterious; it is too all-encompassing; it is too wonderful; it is too intimate – the heart of Our God, revealed to us by Jesus Christ, Our Elder Brother. And they didn't understand the business of God. They thought God would be busy in the synagogue, preaching all day, discussing the Law and the prophets, preoccupied with the Scribes and the Pharisees, the holy and the learned ones. No, the business of God is the ordinary man and woman out there lost, lonely and confused. And my dear friends, remember, every human being stands single and alone before the boundless love of God as if no one else existed.

You and I need to be reminded all the time of God's unfailing, unconditional, eternal love for each of us. It never changes – never! We don't understand that because we are limited, we are finite; we are small-minded; we are sinful. But God never changes in His love for you and me, and He will die ten times all over again rather than that you and I should ever be lost. There is a group of women in the Church called the *Good Shepherds*. They were an association of noble women founded in France by St. John Eudes and Rose-Virginie Pelletier. They spent their lives rehabilitating girls who had gone astray, trying to make them realize that they were loved, that they had a place in life, that they were destined for success, even on this planet; and that their home is beyond the stars. I have worked with them very much over the years and they are truly extraordinary women. But, we owe so much to St. Luke, who in the Fifteenth Chapter of his Gospel, reminds us that when the day is dark and cloudy and we are depressed and discouraged and rejected, we realize the Shepherd never gives up searching for the sheep, the woman never tires of looking for the lost coin, and the Father is waiting with open arms to receive the lost son. Henri Nouwen wrote a marvelous book based on Rembrandt's painting of *The Return of the Prodigal*. It is worth reading. The 17th-century English poet George Herbert said, "The God of Love My Shepherd is, and He it is who does me feed. When He is mine and I am His, what can I want or need?"

Our Lingering Sins

In the Fifth Chapter of St. Matthew's Gospel, we have a fascinating cure. We call it "A Wayside Cure." Our Lord is on His way to cure a twelve-year-old girl, and He meets a woman who had been ill for twelve years. She had been ill ever since the little girl was born, and she had not improved. In fact, she had gotten worse. Now, we think of the woman with her lingering ailments, and we think of ourselves with our lingering sins. Did you and I have a bad temper, ten years ago that brought embarrassment to our family and friends, and dishonor to Christ? Are we any better today? Twelve years ago, were we harboring a grudge that had been done to us long ago? Are we still harboring that grudge? Twelve years ago, were you and I difficult to live with, touchy and hypersensitive? Have we changed? Like the woman, maybe we've grown worse. You see, we do not stay the same. We either go forward or we go backward. At Mass every day, we pray that we may grow in love, with our pope, and with our bishop. And we say the little prayer to the Sacred Heart, "Oh Sacred Heart of Jesus, I implore the grace to love you daily, more and more." Now, the woman in the story who had been ill for twelve years had faith. And she heard about Christ and she was determined to encounter Him. And her faith was so strong; she thought, "If I but touch the hem of His garment, I know I shall be cured." Now my dear friends, for you and for me, our faith demands that we do something about our relationship with Our Lord. He's not going to do for us what He has given us the power to do for ourselves. Are we making an honest effort to try to overcome our problems? I love the story of St. Philip Neri. He was the great Italian saint who founded the Oratorian Congregation, who gave us dear Cardinal Newman. And he was a very wonderful confessor. And one day a woman came to him, and she said, "Father, you know, I talk so easily and so often about my neighbors. I'm always chattering about my neighbors. I'm always judging them, and I shouldn't be like that." He was very kind; he was very understanding; he was very encouraging; he was very sympathetic. And he said, "Now, my dear, for your penance, I want you to go down to the market and buy me a chicken." "Well," she thought, "that's a very intelligent penance. Instead of giving me three Hail Mary's, he has asked me to buy a chicken that he can give to the poor." So, she went to the market and she bought the largest, fattest chicken she could find and she brought it back to St. Philip. And she said, "Father, here is my penance." He said, "Thank you very much. Now, for your penance, I want you to go through the streets of the town plucking the chicken." "Oh, that's real penance, but I deserve it, and I'll do it." And she went off plucking the chicken. And all the people are looking at this crazy lady plucking a chicken out in the street, but she did it. And she finished it, and it was a work of art, and she brought it back to the saint. He said, "Thank you very much. Now, for your penance, I want you to go back and put on the feathers." She said, "What? How can I put on the feathers?" He said, "Why not?" She said, "I don't know where they are. They're blown around everyplace." He said, "Exactly. The words you have uttered are gone from your mouth. You have no control over them. They have been scattered about everywhere. They have been repeated. They have been enlarged, and they are gone forever." She learned her lesson. My dear friends, sanctity is not indolence; it is not laziness; it is not indifference. If you and I are sincere with Our Lord, and we try to be, remember, as I say, as the old theologians used to say, "A Christ not in us is not ours." Christ is in you and in me with His Holy Spirit, to enable us to grow, to become what He intended we should be, because my dear friends, the peace, the serenity, the contentment, the joy, the happiness that you and I crave will be found only in the Lord, only in trying to live with Him and trying to do His Will, in trying keep Him alive on this earth. Remember, He is depending on you and me to keep Him alive, because you and I are here, He is here, and we have one only chance. Our life is limited. For all of us, it is later than we think, and it is our privilege and our joy to surely try to grow in union with Him, Our Elder Brother, and become a child of God as Our Father intended we should be in very truth. And so we pray, "O Lord, show me Your Will and help me to accomplish it. Teach me to do the best thing in the best way, lest I achieve the best thing by unworthy means. I depend on You, My Lord and My God."

Solutions

We read in the First Chapter of St. Matthew's Gospel, the angel of the Lord appeared in a dream to Joseph and said, "Do not be afraid to take Mary as your wife. She has conceived by the Holy Spirit. She shall bring forth a Son and you shall call His Name Jesus, for He shall save His people from their sins" (Matt. 1:20-21). My dear friends, these words sink deep down in the contented Christian soul. You see, the story of the human race is a search for salvation and this is true of commoners and kings, of poets and peasants, of rich and poor, of you and me. We have governments to save us from anarchy; we have police forces to save us from crime; we go to work to be saved from poverty; we go to school to be saved from ignorance and we cultivate our friends to be saved from loneliness. All redeeming experiences begin with relationships. God is relationship - Father, Son, and Holy Spirit. The Father loves the Son, and the Son loves the Father in the Holy Spirit, the Third Person of the Blessed Trinity. And the angel said, "He shall save His people." A relationship has been established between the Lord and you and me because now we are adopted into the family of the Blessed Trinity; we are, in very truth, children of God. On this earth, the relationship that is redeeming begins in the home. There is no substitute for a good home. A child experiences unconsciously the relationship of love between the mother and the father, and the child himself is the object of love and trust and compassion and inspiration. I have a friend who teaches in a prestigious university and he deals with graduate students. And he said to me once, "It is a joy to be able to challenge them because one sees that they were very well-loved." But, my dear friends, you sometimes experience this outside of the home. A young man who has gone bad; he's at war with his family, with the world, with himself. He's in trouble with the law and he's having difficulty in his home. And then suddenly he changes. A young girl comes into his life; she believes in him, she trusts him; she loves him; she inspires him. He's now completely changed; a solid, solid citizen who takes his place in life and becomes very successful. Or in the world of education: a young girl with beauty, with brains, with talent has no interest in learning, no interest in books and a teacher comes out of nowhere and inspires her and opens up to her a world she never knew existed. And she goes on to a great academic career and becomes a wonderful human being because of a relationship. But my dear friends, when the angel said to Joseph, "He shall save His people from their sins," he wasn't talking merely about being saved at the end of our lives of the consequences of our sins, but being saved today, this day, freshly minted from the hand of God, which never came before and will never come again. The old theologians used to say, "A Christ not in us is a Christ not ours." And the Christ in you and in me is going to save us today from where our sins would take us today – our selfishness, our antipathies, our prejudices, our moodiness. Either I control these today with the help of grace or they will control me. Either I will become a shining light in the world today or I will become darkness and a stumbling block to others. You see, sin is in our bloodstream. We were born in sin and you, listening to me now, have been tutored by the years the same as I. You know the struggle we have each day to overcome ourselves, to calm ourselves, to let the Lord take over. But we grow weary and we are lazy and we forget. So, what do we do? We do what all of those who have gone before us did – we turn to Our Lady, the Mother of God. She had no sin. She was not fascinated by evil as you and I are. There was no meanness in Her, only graciousness and love always. And so we say to Her, "O Mary, conceived without sin, pray for us poor sinners in love with our sins, unwilling to give up our sins, wallowing in our sins. Pray for us now at this moment, which is God's gift to us and at the last moment when we leave this world and stand trembling and alone before Your Son."

St. Francis

I am a Franciscan. I am a follower of St. Francis, whom I call my Father in Christ. St. Francis was an extraordinary saint. Everyone in the Western world knows him, even if they don't know much about him. His influence on European art and music and literature has kept scholars happy for a long time. But we are thinking of him as a Christian, as a poor, humble man who tried to follow in the footsteps of Our Lord. You see, Christianity is Christ, and a Christian must try to be a plagiarist of Christ, a shadow of Christ, another Christ. St. Francis is thought to be the truest of Christians, and he lived in the 13th century. He influenced so many people in so many ways of every age and rank that he can truly be called "a man for all seasons, and certainly a man for this season" because the 13th century was not unlike our own. It was the end of an era. There were wars. The feudal system was collapsing. There was restlessness and there was wealth. Francis Bernardone was a child of his age. His parents gave him everything. He knew revelry by night and elegance by day. He had friends, a host of friends, with whom he shared laughter and music and romance. And then suddenly, he grew weary of it all. That sort of life nauseated him and he left home and he became a wanderer. And with this extraordinary intuition, he delved into the riddle and solved the mystery and he discovered the reason for it all was Love – God's love that created everything and sustained everything; God's love that created him and sustained him; the Father from whom he came, to whom he was returning. Now, Francis could never be the same. He saw the Lord 'round every corner of the dusty roads in Italy. New incentives for love everywhere in everything and he cried out, "Love is not loved." He is called the *Il poverello* meaning "the Poor Man." Would it not be more true to call him the rich man – the richest man in the world, because he had the security, the stability, the serenity, the peace that is as immutable as God Himself? Who today, in our restless world, would not give his right arm to have the peace St. Francis had? So many have discovered after searching for it in riches, in pleasure, in amusement that there is still an ache, a void, a loneliness, a longing. They have not found what they were seeking. Francis did. You see, what you and I are seeking is peace that can be found in God alone. My dear friends, you and I cannot live without peace. We need peace for our soul as much as we need air for our body. We cannot even die without peace. For when we will be put in the grave, they will pray that we may rest in peace. Peace is what was promised the night Our Lord was born. "Glory to God in the highest," the angels sang, "and peace on earth to men and women of good will." Peace was the legacy he won for us when He was returning to His Father. "My peace I leave with you, my peace I give to you." Did you ever stop to think of the times we ask for peace during the Mass? And the last thing the priest says is, "The Mass is ended; go in peace." St. Francis is our inspiration in this age. We must learn from him to find the peace we crave. He loved Our Lady. He was the first founder of a religious order to dedicate his order to Our Lady and she is part of our Franciscan heritage. This day, here we are with our weak faith, our inconstant hope and our fitful love and we say the prayer St. Francis composed that we, his sons, say every day. "O great and glorious God and my Lord Jesus Christ, enlighten, I beseech you, the darkness of my mind. Give me a right faith, a firm hope and a constant charity. Grant that I may know You, O Lord, so that always and in all things I may act according to your most holy and perfect Will."

Unfinished Symphony

The German Jesuit theologian Fr. Karl Rahner said, "Most of us die with symphonies unfinished." The symphony, of course, is Christ. We are destined to bring Christ alive each in our own way that is uniquely ours and so often we fail abysmally. My dear friends, while we are on earth, we are to become Christ and play the melody. And the melody is always played in the key of C, because there are no flats and no sharps, and there is a five-finger exercise. The first C is contact. There can be no contact with Our Lord in me without faith. Faith was what Our Lord demanded when He was on earth. He never worked any miracles without faith. It was because of her faith that Magdalene had her sins forgiven. How can you and I go to Confession without faith? Or receive Our Lord in Holy Communion without faith? Or pray without faith? And it isn't how I feel; it's a question of truth and fact. St. Bernard said, "When I feel farthest away from the Lord, then I am nearest to Him." The second C is conflict. I have discovered the Lord within me and now I have to learn His ways and do His Will and that's a conflict because of my selfishness, because of my self-will, because of wanting my own way. The Lord's way doesn't always make sense to me! What am I trying to do at this moment? I wish to make Our Lord known and loved by you. What is the best way to do that? Does He want me to impress you with my Irish gift of gab? Suppose the Lord asked me to fail, unable to put two words together? Am I willing to accept His way? St. Francis said that for him, perfect joy would be to go to a friary and to be attacked by the superior and thrown in the snow and left there for half dead. That for him would be perfect joy because it would bring Our Lord and himself together more really. The 3rd C is conversion and conversation. I forget so easily and so quickly. I need to return to the fact Our Lord is in me wanting to teach me how to live and how to love. And I must remind myself of that a thousand times every day. In all the comings and goings, I must remember I am not alone, I am not lost in the crowd, I mean everything to Him and I must try to allow Him to possess me. And the 4th C is cooperation. That I will cooperate with Him in every way I can. Just as each particle of the Sacred Host contains Our Lord really and truly, so each little happening in my day brings Him to me and brings me to Him if I am aware, if I am sensitive, if I am conscious, if I am truly alive in Him, and try to strengthen the bond. And the final C is contribution. That somehow I will bring something of

His life and His loveliness into the world. Graham Greene wrote a famous play called *The Living Room*, the story of a priest who lived with his two sisters. He was confined to a wheelchair as the result of an accident twenty-five years before. His sisters were very pious, read spiritual books every day. One day their world was shattered because their niece came to live with them. She was not pious; she was not interested in spiritual reading and every afternoon she went out and spent a few hours without coming home. The maid spied on her and she went to the home of the lawyer. They confronted her; she admitted she was in love with him and that she was guilty of sin. The sisters were horrified. They asked her to leave their home. Before she did, she went in to her uncle the priest and she sobbed out her story. Later he said, "All she should have had to do was to come into my presence to find the Lord. She came seeking hope; all she found was despair. She came seeking Him and all she found was me." St. Francis told his friars to preach, and to use words if they needed. My dear friends, the symphony that you and I have to achieve on this earth is to try to bring the Lord alive each in our own way. And surely the prayer of Cardinal Newman, which was the prayer of Mother Teresa and the prayer of many noble men and women, is our prayer. "Teach me, O Lord, to bring you alive. Flood my soul with Your Spirit and life. Penetrate and possess my whole being so utterly that all my life may be only a radiance of Thine. Shine through me and be so in me that every soul I come in contact with may feel your presence in my soul. Let them look up and see no longer me, but only Jesus."

Sermon on the Mount

The great French writer André Gide wrote a short story once, called
The Pastoral Symphony. It was the story of Gertrude, who was
born blind. And in her blindness, she forged a great attraction to
people. Years later, in an operation, her sight was restored and she
made two tremendous discoveries – the extraordinary beauty of
nature and the sadness of human beings. Sometimes she wished
she had never regained her sight. Well, Our Lord saw the sadness
of human beings, too, because they put their happiness in material
things and He gave the formula for blessedness for us all. We have
it in the Fifth Chapter of St. Matthew, called the *Sermon on the
Mount*, and the Sixth Chapter of St. Luke, called the *Sermon on
the Plain*. "Blessed are the poor in spirit, the Kingdom of Heaven
is theirs. Blessed are those who mourn, they shall be comforted.
Blessed are the meek, they shall possess the land. Blessed are
those who hunger and thirst for holiness, they shall have their fill.
Blessed are the merciful, they shall obtain mercy. Blessed are the
clean of heart, they shall see God. Blessed are the peacemakers,
they shall be called the children of God. And blessed are they who
suffer persecution for righteousness, the Kingdom of Heaven is
theirs" (Matt. 5:3-10). Not once does He mention houses or money
or fame or power or prestige or exciting entertainment or exotic
cruises to faraway places with strange-sounding names. These are
the things that we foolishly imagine will bring us happiness. Not
to say that the change of circumstances for many people would not
be a big improvement. But how difficult it is for you and me not to
think that if we had a bigger house, if we moved to the other side
of town, if we had a better job, if only we could win the lottery
once – all these things. But Augustine discovered a long time ago,

"You have made us for Yourself, O Lord, and our heart will ever be restless until it rests in you." Oscar Wilde said, "There are two terrible tragedies in life. One is not to get what you set your heart on and the other, to get it." Some of us discover this the hard way. But what does He mean by "Blessed are the poor in spirit, for the Kingdom of God is theirs already?" St. Paul told the Philippians in the Second Chapter of his Epistle, "Let this mind be in you, which was in Christ Jesus, who, although He was God, emptied Himself, taking the form of a servant" (Phil. 2:5-7). Poverty of spirit means that I am empty. You know as well as I that nature abhors a vacuum and we have to be filled with something. We are usually filled with persons, places and things. And tragically, we do not own them; they own us. And it is the struggle every day to keep myself free so that the Lord can possess me. Benedict Joseph Labré was a great saint. He tried to be a Trappist on a couple of occasions and the religious life was too great a challenge for him. He was a beggar man in Rome and he used to sleep at night in the Coliseum. And every night he moved from place to place lest he become attached to one particular place. You and I, my dear friends, have to learn to let go; to let go of yesterday; to let go of our youth; to let go of the joys and happiness of our growing years. So many of us live in the past or in the future. We must enjoy God's gift to us today. That's why we call it "the present." And my dear friends, in your life and mine with its drudgery, its sameness, its monotony, rubbing shoulders with the same dreary depressed people day after day, we must learn to face all these challenges with Our Lord, finding our strength, our staying power in Him as we are emptied of everything except Him. There isn't much you and I can do for Him, but He wants us to do everything with Him. We are always beginning. Let's try again and let our prayer be the prayer of the saints and those who have gone before us. "Oh Jesus, meek and humble of heart, make my heart like unto Thine."

The Blessed Sacrament

"O Sacrament most holy, O Sacrament divine, all praise and all thanksgiving be every moment Thine." These words are said and sung in every church in the country on Holy Thursday, on the Feast of Corpus Christi and during the Forty Hours. And now as a result of the Pope's suggestion, there is a new awareness of the Blessed Sacrament in churches throughout the land. They have Perpetual Adoration in many parishes. When you and I come into the presence of the Blessed Sacrament, we are in Heaven on earth. For what do the angels and saints have in Heaven that you and I do not have here? We have the very same God. What will Heaven be for you and me one day but the unveiling of the Blessed Sacrament, the seeing of Him in all His dazzling beauty, in all His loveliness and all His glory. I mentioned the name of Fr. Frederick William Faber earlier. He was an English convert to the Church in the middle of the 19th century. He joined the Congregation of the Oratory founded by St. Philip Neri and became the Superior of the Brompton Oratory in London, while Cardinal Newman was the Superior of the Oratory in Birmingham. Fr. Faber said wonderful things about the Blessed Sacrament. "What a gift we have in the Blessed Sacrament," he said. "What a vision of the Divine Magnificence it is." "'Tis the sun and center of our mysteries, the food of our souls, the inspiration of our art, the magnet of the whole Church." And yet for what end do men and women seem to use this priceless gift of God but to make the wound in His Sacred Heart wider. For what is the life of Our Lord in the Blessed

116

Sacrament but a life of suffering. All through the passing years He's here in our midst, suffering. Mystically, it is true, but nonetheless it is really true. And we never give Him a thought. We go on our way unthinkingly. Oh, we pray sometimes, but do we mean what we say? "With desolation the whole world is made desolate," the prophet said, "because there are so few who think in their hearts." Let's think for a brief moment on some of the sufferings of Our Lord in the Blessed Sacrament. Was there ever helplessness like to His? The immense space of the wide heavens is His. Freedom and power and joy belong to Him as to no one else. There is not an intellect that knows, a mind that reasons, a heart that beats, except through, from and in Him. Why, the bedridden patients in our hospitals have far more power over themselves than the King of Glory whom Love has caught in the meshes of this Sacrament. And He's our prisoner under lock and key. At stated times we take Him out to show Him to the people to prove He has not escaped. How our Captive God loves us! One can almost hear Him say, "Oh, foolish, thoughtless children, if you will not worship me as your Omnipotent God, at least pity me as your helpless prisoner." Our Lord isn't only a prisoner, He's a slave. Yet he remains King of Kings, Lord of Lords, Maker of Land and Sea. He waves His scepter over eternity, over millions of uncreated and created worlds. Yet He has flung them all away in order to come to plead for the kingdom, to free men's hearts. He will go on pleading until the end of days. There is no length to which He will not go, no depth to which He will not descend to win the love of your heart and mine. He knew that men and women could love Him and that they could inspire one another to love Him and each other with grateful generosity. But what about the unvisited Lord in our tabernacles? In our world of crowded streets, busy theaters, frantic comings and goings, what about the Lord who lives in the Church down the street; who remains alone and forgotten. When we do we visit Him, what do we say? In the 13th century, St. Thomas Aquinas said it all. "O Godhead hid, devoutly I adore Thee, who truly art within these forms before me, to Thee my head I bow with bended knee as failing quite in contemplating Thee." We come to Him our Father, our judge with whom we are going to spend our eternity, our companion in our exile. And we say with all the noble men and women who have gone before us, "May the heart of Jesus in the most Blessed Sacrament be praised, adored, and loved with grateful affection at every moment in all the tabernacles of the world, even to the end of time."

Who Are We?

We know St. John the Evangelist as the Beloved Disciple. He was the brother of St. James. They were called the Sons of Thunder. You remember, their mother wanted them to sit at the right and left hand of the Lord when He came into His Kingdom. St. John is known as "the beloved disciple" because he was the friend of Our Lord, sat next to Him at the Last Supper and leaned on His shoulder. He wrote the Fourth Gospel and he wrote two Epistles. In the first of his Epistles, he said an extraordinary thing – that we, you and I, are "children of God." Our Lord said three things that startled the Jews, that they could not accept, for which He gave His Life – that God is not solitary, that He's Three-in-One, Father, Son and Holy Spirit; second, that He was the Son of the Father; and thirdly, that you and I are destined to be children of God, heirs to the Kingdom of Heaven. We know we are sinners, you and I. We demonstrate that brilliantly, a thousand times every day. But Our Lord sees in us the potential for greatness. He saw it in the human beings He encountered when He was on earth. You remember His encounter with the woman taken in adultery. She was dragged before Him. "She should be stoned," they said. But Our Lord saw in her the potential for greatness and true love. Can you imagine the conversation they had, He and the poor woman? And she went away from Him inspired, uplifted, ennobled when He said to her, "Sin no more. Go in peace." And His encounter with Simon Peter – Simon, the arrogant one, the impetuous one, the strange one – He said to him, "Your name is Peter. You are the rock on which I shall build My Church." Not, "You should be the rock," or "You ought to be the rock," or "You will be the rock;" but "You are the rock on which I will build My Church." Whoever you are listening to me now, however weary or discouraged or ashamed, remember your dignity. As St. Leo said, "You are a child of God." Christ appeared on this earth 2,000 years ago, and all He had was His character and His teaching, and the world has never been able to forget Him. Did you ever stop to think, "If Christ had not come on this earth, we would have no paintings of Giotto, or Cimabue. We would have no *Missa Solemnis* of Beethoven; we would have no Handel's *Messiah* with its "Alleluia Chorus"; there would be no San Francisco or Los Angeles. There would be no Santa Fe; there would be no St. Louis; there would be no San Antonio; there would be no St. Patrick's Cathedral in New York, all because of Christ's coming to this earth. And He is our elder brother. And you and I have been made one with Him. We need to be reminded. We need to hear again and again that we are a child of God; that God is Our Father; that Christ is our Elder Brother, and that the Spirit of God lives in the depth of our being. I read a story of an eagle that was hatched with chickens. And the eagle grew up with the chickens and ate with the chickens and behaved like the chickens and thought it was a chicken. And one day, it saw an eagle flying in the sky and thought, "Oh, how I would love to be able to do that." And then it was reminded that it was an eagle. You and I are eagles. We must never forget our destiny. My dear friend, do you ever stop to think of your destiny? Listen to what is said in the Book of Revelation. "You shall see God face-to-face. His name will be written on your forehead. It will never be night again. You will not need lamplight or sunlight, because the Lord God will be shining on you and you will reign forever and ever" (Rev. 22:4). This is your destiny. And while you are down here on your journey home, remember the Lord your God is living within you, to sustain you, to uphold you, to inspire you, to encourage you. If we forget this, we are in deep spiritual trouble. We must remember who we are, children of God destined for glory. And surely the prayer of Archbishop Gutierre is yours and mine. "O Lord, I need you for myself. I am poor; I am needy; I am sinful. I need you for your sake so that I may know you, so that I may love you. I need you for the sake of others that I may do them no harm, that I may bring you to them."

The Banquet of God

Is it long since you've been to a formal banquet? Perhaps the last time was the prom at your graduation? But you remember the dress or the suit you wore and the person who went with you and the flowers you had? Perhaps you still have some of them, pressed between the pages of a book. They are nice memories. The poet said, "God gave us memory so that we can have roses in December." In the Twenty-Second Chapter of St. Matthew's Gospel, Our Lord likens the Kingdom of God to a banquet – a banquet the King gave for His Son. Everything was ready, the food was cooked, and He sent His servants out with invitations. But a strange thing happened – some refused the invitation, others insulted the servants. This was clear, of course, as a warning to the Jews of the time. But it is a symbol of life and the Kingdom of God for us. Young people do not always understand what is involved in a formal banquet – someone has to plan the menu, someone has to cook the food, someone has to lay the tables, and then someone has to clean up when it's all over. I was reading recently about a lady in New York who goes to work at night cleaning offices in a large office building. She has a lovely personality, and as people are going home at night, she has a cheery, "Goodnight; pleasant dreams!" Her birthday was coming and they decided it would be nice to give her a party. And a CEO in one of the offices said, "You can have my suite." And they all got together and told her they were going to give her a party. And she said, "Thank you, but no thank you. Because when you all go home, I'll have to clean up." But my dear friends, life is like a banquet. We are invited into life, and things are prepared – the air, the water, and the sunlight. And we're invited to an education, young people are. The schools are there, the teachers are there, the libraries filled with books are there, and the wisdom of the ages is there for the asking. But, of course, invitations don't last forever. Unless they are used, there is an expiration date. But my dear friends, we are invited into the Kingdom of God. We are adopted into God's family. I am sure that some of you, like me, are adopted. We have been adopted into the United States of America. And I have been adopted by the Franciscans of New York in Holy Name Province. And all through the years I have been adopted into monasteries and convents and rectories as each week I preached the Word of God and lived with those under the same roof and became part of the family. But for you and me to be adopted into the family of God and to be an heir of His Kingdom, when you and I receive Jesus Christ in Holy Communion, we can truly, literally say, "Our Father." Jesus Christ and I have the same Father. He is my Elder Brother. In the Third Chapter of Revelations, the last book of the Bible, we read Our Lord saying, "Behold, I stand at the door and knock. If anyone open to Me, I shall come in and dine with him" (Rev. 3:20). Holman Hunt, the English artist who painted this, had his little son looking at him and saying, "Dad, why doesn't He go in?" And the artist said, "Son, the latch is on the inside." The Lord invites you and me, and asks us to let Him come and dine with us, to become a member of the family, as He makes us a member of His Family. But in the story Our Lord told, someone was found at the banquet that did not have a wedding garment. Now, to be adopted into the family of God means I must become a child of God, not in word and in tongue, but in deed and in truth. I must be clothed with Christ. I must put on Christ. In the famous Thirteenth Chapter of St. Paul's First Epistle to the Corinthians, there is the description of love. "Love is patient, love is kind..."(1 Cor. 13:4). Now, if you substitute the word *Christ* for *Love*, you have it: "Christ is patient, Christ is kind. He feels no envy." But now you substitute the word "yourself," "Mary," "John." "Mary is kind, she feeds no envy, she is never perverse or proud, she does not brood over an injury, she plays no havoc in wrongdoing, but rejoices at the victory of truth, sustains, hopes, endures to the end," that's the garment that you and I must wear before we can enter Heaven, and that's the challenge of our lives. And so, we pray, "O Lord, help me to love you with all my heart, with all my soul, with all my strength, with all my mind, because if I do not, I shall have lesser loves. Help me to put you first, so that you will be My Love, My Hope, and My final Joy."

How to Handle Worry

In the Twenty-First Chapter of St. Luke's Gospel, Our Lord takes an honest look at the fearful and uncertain side of life. He was trying to prepare His followers for the difficult days that were ahead. But today He is speaking to you and to me. He never promised us a rose garden, but He knows that worry in human beings. Anxiety about the future probably does more damage to human beings than wars and hurricanes combined. No wonder we say at Mass every day, after the *Our Father* and before the Holy Communion, "Preserve us, Lord, from all anxiety as we wait in joyful hope for the coming of Our Savior, Jesus Christ." But how do you and I handle worry? Let me remind you, you who are listening to me of God's love for you. He never promised to keep us from trouble, but to sustain us in the midst of trouble. Not one hair of our head will be harmed and not even death can harm someone who trusts in God. Someone who believes in God has power over life or death into eternity. And we must be sure not to worry about the things we cannot change. What can you and I do about the weather or about wars and earthquakes? Surely, we must learn to accept. *The Serenity Prayer* makes great sense. "Give me, O Lord, the courage to change the things I can, the serenity to accept the things I can't – and the wisdom to know the difference." And we ought to live in the here and now. Today is all we have. "Give us this day our daily bread," we pray. "Take no thought for tomorrow," He said. When you and I believe that God loves us and He is with us and that we are never alone, surely we can say with St. Paul, "I can do all things in Him who strengthens me." And my dear friends, we must learn to keep small things small. Do we? Look at the way we so often magnify trivial things and so lose our equilibrium and our peace. As you and I are here right now, connected through God's gift of television, what are the priorities in our lives? They are basic rules of Christianity for every child of God and they are five in number. They are like the five-finger exercises you learned when playing the piano. You can say them driving your car; you can say them waiting for a bus; you can say them standing in line at the counter in the supermarket; and you can say them before you sleep at night. First, God loves you and me with a love we cannot even begin to imagine – a love that is constant, unwavering, always, in spite of our infidelity and our sin. Secondly, He is living, truly living in us, at every moment of the day and night so that we can say with St. Paul, "I live no longer I; it is Christ Who lives in me." Thirdly, moment-by-moment, we are traveling together, He and I. Some years ago, a book was published; it was the diary of a French woman. It became a best-seller and theologians lauded it for its wisdom. She called it, *He and I* – the inner life she lived with Our Lord every day and the peace and happiness she enjoyed. Fourthly, our home is not here; it's in Heaven! We are going back to the God from Whom we came and our place is there now, waiting for us. And finally, death will be our loveliest moment because it will begin an ecstasy of joy that will never end. Surely, with St. Francis, "Welcome, Sister Death." My dear friends, as we think on these five truths, surely we stammer out with the man in the Gospel from the depths of our being, "Lord, I believe. Help Thou my unbelief."

REFLECTIONS V

A Name, Not a Number

As you know in our world today, numbers predominate more and more. You have a phone number, a house number, an apartment number, a zip code, and a Social Security number. There is the danger that names are forgotten. How different in the Bible. The Bible is full of names, some of them unpronounceable but very real to God. In Psalm 147, we are told that God knows the number of the stars and calls each one by name. In the Twelfth Chapter of St. Luke, Our Lord tells the 72 disciples on their return from their first mission to rejoice, because their names are written in Heaven. Now, God doesn't need to write names to remember them. We forget names. God never does. The only thing God forgets is our sins that have been forgiven. I remember hearing about a woman to whom Christ was appearing and she experienced great peace and great joy but she was afraid that maybe it wasn't real. So she went to the bishop. She had known him since the day he was pastor in her parish. She was a mature woman, the mother of a family, and he had great respect for her. And she told him of these appearances of the Lord. And she said to him, "Do you think they are real?" And he said, "I know what I'll do." He said, "The next time Christ appears to you, ask Him what was my besetting sin, my predominant fault before I became a bishop." She said she would and when she came the next time he said, "Did you ask Our Lord?" She said, "Yes, I did." And what did He say? He smiled at me and said, "I have forgotten." That's Our God. That's the love we do not understand, the love that envelops you and me every moment of the day and night. In the New Testament in St. Luke at the beginning, the angel appears and says, "Do not be afraid, Mary; you have found favor with God. You shall conceive and bear a Son and you shall call His Name *Jesus* because He will save His people from their sins." Christ called Simon and changed his name to Peter. He called Saul and changed his name to Paul. You remember the tax collector, the little man Zacchaeus, who heard Christ was passing by and went up in a tree to see Him. The Lord stopped and looked up and called, "Zacchaeus, come down. I'm coming to your home today." Did you ever imagine yourself in that position, when the Lord would call your name? I often think of it. If He called my name, I wouldn't come down, I'd fall down dead! We are told in the Second Chapter of Revelation that each of us were given a name by God when He created us. When He calls that name at our death, we will recognize it and return to Him faster than sound. God not only created you and me as unique persons, but gave us each a name. He has also given us a work to do, one that no one else can do. Cardinal Newman spoke brilliantly, inspiringly about it saying, "If I am in sickness, my sickness will praise Him. If I fail, my failure can praise Him." God can do everything. All will work together unto good. I am thinking of the story of Leonard Cheshire, an English pilot in World War II. He was an agnostic. One night after a bombing expedition in Germany, he returned weary and went into the Officers' Mess for a drink. The officers were there with their girlfriends having a drink and he ordered a drink. And while he was waiting he heard a girl say to her boyfriend, "God is not a moral notion. He is a Person. He is my best friend. I talk to Him every day." Leonard Cheshire never heard that before – God is a person, his best friend. He went out and he thought about this. It haunted him. He went to the library and he read and in his own way he prayed and finally he became a Catholic and he founded the Cheshire Homes that are all over the world today. Who was the girl in the bar? He had no idea. He never saw her. Can you imagine their meeting in Heaven and him saying to her, "Thank you." And she will say, "For what? I never met you in my life." He'll say "No, but the words you uttered changed my life forever." And this is the way God works with all of us. You and I will never know when our loveliest moment will strike. But He will know. He will take care of everything. And so, my dear friends, surely the words of Isaiah in the Forty-Third Chapter find an echo in our hearts. "Fear not, you are mine. I have redeemed you. I have called you by name. You are mine" (Isa. 43:1)

God's Will

In the First Chapter of St. Luke's Gospel, we find God in action, mysteriously, in the first century of our world. His program does not involve any military might or political power. Rather, the meeting of two pregnant women somewhere in Judea. One, Elizabeth, was older. She was to give birth to John the Baptist, the greatest man ever born of woman. The other was young, the most beautiful woman in God's creation, Mary, Our Lady, who was to give birth to Jesus Christ, Our Companion in our exile, Our Savior and Our God. God's ways did not involve any summit meeting in Palestine

or Geneva or the convening of any giant corporation. It was just
these two women, unknown to the world. The world did not know
or could not care what was happening in that Judean place. God
works quietly. This is very evident in the Old Testament. We read
in the Ninth Chapter of the Third Book of Kings, how Elijah was
having one of those days when he was tired of living and scared of
dying. He was running away from the wicked queen Jezebel and
then God intervened. There was a mighty wind, which loosened the
very rocks; but God was not heard in the wind. Then there was an
earthquake, which shook everything to its foundations; but God was
not in the earthquake. Then there was a fire, but God was not in the
fire. But finally, there was a gentle breeze and God spoke to Elijah
in the breeze. Have you ever stood in a country lane and watched
the dawn – that irrepressible light that puts the darkness to flight and
then envelops the whole world? There are no trumpet blares; no
banners are unfurled. It is quiet; it is real; it is awesome. In Florida,
in Key West, every evening when the sun sets at the most southerly
point of the continent, people gather there in hushed silence as they
watch the sun descend beyond the horizon. And then, instinctively,
they burst into applause, because this is truly the greatest show on
Earth. My dear friends, you and I are so accustomed to noise and
ballyhoo, we forget that God really speaks to us in the stillness of a
sleepless night, alone before the Blessed Sacrament in the quiet of a
church, or in the secret recesses of our own heart. I am remembering
that on an ordinary day in an ordinary church, an ordinary priest read
the Gospel of St. Matthew and Francis Bernadone was listening,
and his life was changed forever. And God uses small things. In
that first century, everybody thought that what was happening in
Caesar's palace was important. Oh no! It's what was happening in

Mary's womb. I am remembering Europe at the beginning of the last century. Napoleon was a world power. They trembled at the sound of his name from the Danube to the Rhine. In 1809, he was so powerful. We forget the majesty of Napoleon. He dared to kidnap the Pope! Yes, he made the Holy Father prisoner and compelled him to crown himself as emperor. In 1809, people were thinking that what was important in the world was what was happening in the emperor's palace. No. In 1809, what was happening that was important was the birth of babies. That year, Abraham Lincoln was born and William Gladstone and Tennyson and Mendelssohn and a host of other people. We have long since forgotten the triumphs of Napoleon; but the world, for a long, long time, will be remembering the babies who were born in the year 1809. My dear friends, we are living in an extraordinary era, by God's plan, you and I. And we are witnessing extraordinary miracles before our very eyes. One of them is EWTN. When God wanted to make His self known throughout the world, He did not choose a giant corporation, or some famous cardinals in His Church, or some wonderful preachers. He chose a contemplative nun in her convent, who spent herself and allowed herself to be spent, that the God Whom she worshipped would be known in every corner of the world. And in ways she could not have imagined, none of us could have imagined, Mother Angelica's prayer was heard. And now, EWTN is in the four corners of the globe. May God be praised! But my dear friends, in our own lonely lives, do we sometimes think that when we have grey days and dark nights, that God has forgotten His world and forgotten us? How we need to be reminded again and again, that you and I stand before Our God as if we were the only human beings; that He loves you and me as if there were no one else on earth; and that He died for you and me, and is willing to die ten times all over again rather than we should ever be lost. How we need to hear this. How we need to delve into mystery, which is inexhaustible. How we ask His Spirit of Love to bring it to our minds when we become discouraged and depressed. So, we say to Him on this lovely day, "Oh Lord, Our Father and Our God, help us to understand in a new way that Your love is the great reality in our lives and that your dealings with us, with each one of us, are filled with love. Maybe we will not understand it during our pilgrimage, but we will spend our eternity praising you for the love that enveloped us all our days."

On Talking To Ourselves

We sometimes joke about people who talk to themselves. The truth is, it is something we all of us do and there are few things we do that are more important. Every movement we make is a result of a conversation we've had with ourselves. Virtually everything we do today is the result of talking to ourselves yesterday. In the Twelfth Chapter of St. Luke's Gospel, Our Lord tells us about a man who talked to himself. He suddenly came into much wealth and asked himself the question, "What shall I do? I shall pull down my barns and build larger ones." And then he took an appraisal of the situation. He said, "You have many blessings in store for yourself." And he finally gave himself some advice, "Relax, eat heartily, drink merrily, and enjoy yourself." Our Lord said that man was a fool. First of all, he didn't know that he was going to die that very night; but secondly, he was foolish because of his selfishness. Everything was "I," "me," "mine." There was no mention of another member of his family or friends, of neighbors, and certainly not of God. But it was God who gave him the riches; God Who gave him his strength, energy and acumen. It was God who blessed the harvest. Here he was now telling himself four things – "I am going to relax; I am going to eat well; I am going to drink much; and I am going to enjoy life." He was wrong because money could buy food and drink but money could not buy a clear conscience. Money could not buy the affection, love and respect of other people. Today money is the ideal, the standard by which people judge, and this is wrong. I remember reading about a priest in a large, affluent parish and a few Sundays before Christmas, he said to the good people in church, "I know you're all very busy buying gifts one for another for Christmas. Did you ever stop to think that you could buy a gift for Christ? I know where He lives. If you'll come next Sunday, I shall tell you." So, next Sunday the church was crowded as people came to find out where Our Lord lived on earth. And the priest went into the pulpit with a thousand cards that had the names and addresses of people who were sick and poor and lonely. Remember what Our Lord said to us in the Twenty-Fifth Chapter of St. Matthew's Gospel, "What you do to those around you, you do to me." But you and I are different from the man in the Gospel because we are children of God. God Our Father has given us, not only His Beloved Son: but His own Spirit, the Spirit of God. The Spirit that took Our Lord into the desert, the Spirit of Love that took Our Lord to Calvary. That same Spirit is living in you and in me; and don't you remember His gifts – wisdom, understanding, counsel, fortitude, knowledge, piety, and the fear of the Lord? Prayer is not only talking to the Lord, it's also listening to Him. And the spirit of wisdom in you and in me will inspire us to do the right thing that will give glory to the Father. And so, my dear friends, surely this old Irish blessing finds an echo in our hearts. "May the Grace of Christ uphold you. May the Father's love enfold you. May the Holy Spirit guide you with joy and peace now and to eternity."

One Day at a Time

In Psalm 118 we read this wonderful line, "This is the day the Lord has made... let us be glad and rejoice in it." God makes every day freshly minted from His Hand in love, given to you and to me so that we may find Him and find our fulfillment in finding Him today. You remember when He went to the synagogue in Nazareth for the first time and read from the Book of Isaiah. He said to the people, "This day, this reading has been fulfilled in your ears." And you remember the day He said to Zachaeus, "Today I am going to dine in your home." And what He said to the Good Thief when he was dying on the cross, we hope and pray He will say to you and me, "This day you will be with me in Paradise." We are asked to live only for one day. At the end of the day we rehearse for death and sleep and we put down our cross. Did you ever stop to think what a blessing, what a mercy it is that we see our life day-by-day? Can you imagine taking a carpenter up on a helicopter and showing him five miles of houses and saying to him, "These are what you have to build in your lifetime?" Or can you imagine filling Madison Square Garden in New York with the sick and the dying and saying to any doctor or nurse, "These are the people you have to nurse during your lifetime?" Or take any housewife and show her a mountain of dishes to be cleaned? No, God is very good to us that we just see our life only one day at a time. But why don't we enjoy every day that God gives us? What is the problem for you and for me? Ah my dear friend, it's the age-old problem of sin. We are sinners. We are selfish, unconsciously demanding human beings, and we want it our way and we kick against the goad all the time. In the Sixth Chapter of St. Matthew's Gospel, Our Lord said, "If your eye is single, your whole body will be lightsome" (Matt. 7:22). It's the eye of my soul from which I look at life and people. It is the way I judge that causes my problems. I am prejudiced; I am jealous; I am highly sensitive. That is the way we are made, sinners, and we have to struggle all the time, every hour of every day to try and see the hand of God in our lives and the hand of God is love. "All things work together unto good for those who love God." You remember in the Old Testament when the Jews were wandering in the Promised Land, God fed them with manna but they got only enough for one day. And He taught us to pray, "Give us this day our daily Bread." Take no thought for tomorrow. Today that God has given me, this day that is filled with love and filled with Him – He wants me to enjoy. You see, my dear friends, in Heaven there is only love. And you and I are on this earth for a few fleeting years to learn to love so that when we come to die we will be fit to enter Heaven where there is only love. It's the challenge we have to face every single day while we have God's own Spirit within us to help us, to make of today something worthwhile and memorable. Surely the lines of the old hymn with the haunting melody find an echo in your heart today. "This day God sends me with strength for my steersman, His might to uphold me, His wisdom to guide, His ears are listening, His eyes are watchful, His lips are speaking, dear friend at my side."

How We Handle Our Failures

One of the common denominators of our race is a sense of moral failure. We have a standard by which we try to live. We have an idea and a dream by which we measure ourselves and we are conscious when we fail. This is not a gloomy picture; it's a compliment because among all God's creatures we're the only ones who have a sense of right or wrong. This is not true of the little dog sitting on your lap or nestling at your feet right now as you're listening to me. It's not true of the cow or the horse; they are not aware that they are less than they should be. This is your privilege and mine. And the question is, "What do we do with your failures and our mistakes?" We think of St. Peter and St. Paul. They took full responsibility for their failures and by the grace of God they turned them into benefits. Remember who St. Peter was. He was given a vision of Heaven on Mount Tabor and said, "Lord, it is good for us to be here; let us remain here always." And he then denied His Lord three times. He swore he did not know Him. He said, "Depart from me, O Lord. I am a sinful man." St. Paul said, "I am the least of the Apostles. I am not worthy to be called an apostle because I persecuted the Church." He held the clothes of those who stoned St. Stephen, our first martyr. And by the grace of God they turned their moral failures to their benefits. Suppose they made excuses. Now, there were evil forces active in their lives as there are evil forces active in yours and mine. Suppose St. Peter said, "I am a sinner, of course I'm a sinner! Everyone around me is a sinner. Look at where I was born, on the water's edge, in the midst of rough men. I learned to curse and to fight as soon as I learned to walk and to talk. It's the fault of my parents and of my community." If he had said this there might have been some truth in it but he would never have been the man to whom Our Lord said, "You are the rock on whom I'm going to build my Church." We would never have heard of him unless he had admitted his failures. And this is the glory of the Lord and the glory of the Church He founded that through his priests, every one of us can have our sins obliterated forever. Gilbert Keith Chesterton, who came into the Church way back in the 1920's and wrote a marvelous book that you should read sometime called *Orthodoxy*, said, "Now that I am gray and gouty, I need to have my sins forgiven, and where on earth can they be forgiven except in the Catholic Church." And what a success he made of his life as a Catholic. One thinks of all those addicted to drugs and to drink who, by the grace of God, changed their lives. One thinks of Francis Thompson, the poet who wrote *The Hound of Heaven*. He was a seminarian; he left the seminary and became a drug addict on the streets of London. And then he wrote, "I fled him down the nights and down the days; I fled him down the arches of the years; I fled him down the labyrinthine ways of my own mind," and then he heard Him say, "Who will love ignoble thee save Me, save only Me?" And he made a huge success of his life. One thinks of all those who were slaves to the flesh and by the grace of God changed their lives. One thinks of Margaret of Cortona at the grave of her dead lover, a man with whom she had lived for years. At his graveside the Lord spoke to her and she said to Him, "Lord, You have conquered me. I am Yours." She is a canonized saint. One thinks of Augustine who prayed, "Lord, give me purity but not yet." And then he wrote, "You have made us for yourself, O Lord, and our hearts will be ever restless until they rest in you." And we have the same Lord and the same grace and the same Church at our disposal. We must take full responsibility for our failures. Admit them to Our Lord and hear his words of absolution. Surely the words of Psalm 63 find an echo in our hearts, "Oh God, You are My God. For You I long; for you my soul is thirsting; my body pines for you like a dry and weary land without water because your love is better than life."

Reminders

How true it is that people do not need to be instructed as much as to be reminded. We need to be reminded again and again of what Jesus Christ, the Second Person of the Blessed Trinity, has done for you and me. We need to hear again what it means to be a Catholic, a member of the Mystical Body. Our Lord came down here to make you listen to God really and truly in Him. He gives us His body, blood, soul, and divinity really and truly. He is living in us. One hundred and fifty-five times in the Epistles of St. Paul the two little words "in Christ" occur. And St. Paul boasts, "I live no longer I, Christ lives in me; for me to live is Christ." This is an extraordinary mystery that you and I are truly children of God in Christ. He came to give us His life. "I have come that you may have life and have it more abundantly. I am the Life." Coursing through your veins and mine is the eternal, unending, dynamic life of the Blessed Trinity of God Himself, the life that you and I will live for all eternity. And as you know, life, by definition, must be lived. St. Irenaeus way back in the second century said, "The glory of God is a human being radiantly alive." God help us, most of us are half dead! We are not radiantly alive as God intends we should be. We allow that life to stay in us unused, unlived and because we have God's life in us, God is Our Father. You are sitting here listening to me now with a thousand stray thoughts on your mind – with your worries, your fears, your insecurity, your loneliness – and God Your Father is madly in love with you. He never had to create you. He created you for a purpose and He is there with His Son and the Holy Spirit living in you. And He is My Father in a way that no one else can be, because there's an intimacy in our relationship that is mysterious and unique. He came to give you His merits. This is mind-boggling:

the merits of Our Lord's death are for you, as if no one else existed. This is the glory of the Mass; that we go to Calvary and we offer our dreary lives to God with Christ, through Christ, and in Christ. There is the lovely symbolism of the drop of water plunged into the wine. It symbolizes you and me: small, weak, unimportant, hardly noticeable, becoming one with Our Lord. And God accepts the merits of His Son as if you and I had died. And finally, He gives us His home. "I have gone to prepare a place for you so that where I am you also may be." So that you and I are truly heirs to the Kingdom of Heaven in Jesus Christ. Many years ago when I was a young priest, I was asked to give a retreat to the Sisters in Hertfordshire in England. They ran a famous school for girls. After graduation the girls came back to visit the Sisters because they loved them. One of their girls became a nurse. During the war she served overseas with the British Army and she fell in love with an enlisted man. He was young, small and very thin. He could hardly be classed as handsome. But he had impeccable manners. He was a charming human being and she fell madly in love with him. They got married in France and they had their friends as witnesses. Then he brought her home to England and she discovered he was a Lord of the Manor. He had endless wealth, servants, a mansion and vast land holdings. But he never told her about any of this, because he wanted her to marry him for himself. Her reaction to all of this – she cried. She could not stop crying. And the sisters brought her to me because they didn't know how to handle the situation. When you and I arrive in Heaven and see what Our Elder Brother has prepared for us, we will be speechless with joy and tears of joy - for all eternity. The wonderful prayer of Cardinal Newman is the prayer of each one of us. "Dear Jesus, help me to spread your fragrance everywhere I go. Flood my soul with Your Spirit and life. Penetrate and possess my whole being so utterly that all my life may be only a radiance of Thine. Shine through me and be so in me that every soul I come in contact with may feel your presence in my soul. Let them look up and see no longer me but only Jesus. The light, O Lord, will be all from you; none of it will be mine."

The Importance of One Person

In the Sixth Chapter of St. John's Gospel, we have the famous miracle of Our Lord that you all know – the miracle of the loaves and fishes. After Our Lord, the important person in the story is the little peasant boy who comes with his lunch. We presume he was a peasant boy because he had a peasant's lunch. And he glides in and out of the Gospel to remind us of the importance of one person. We don't know precisely how many people were there on that day. The Gospel tells us there were five thousand men. I presume their wives came, too, and some of their children. As a result of this day's outing, the little peasant boy discovered he was important. So are we. If only we could know this and remember this, we are important to our God. The peasant boy reminds us of the uniqueness of each individual. He was there among all the people, but He had something no one else had. He had lunch, and that lunch saved the day for everybody. He was unique. Sometimes we seem to be lost in the crowd. We think we are just another person, but each one of us is unique. We have a saying in the Western world that when God created some people, He threw away the mold. When God created Florence Nightingale or Helen Keller, He threw away the mold; or when He created Abraham Lincoln or Napoleon, He threw away the mold. When He created you, He threw away the mold. You are not a carbon copy; you're an original! And this peasant boy reminds us of the importance of every person. Remember, that young growing boy would have been hungry. He could have said, "This is my lunch and I need it." But he gave it to St. Andrew. He must have had a good mother who taught him to give and to share. Or perhaps he went to the synagogue with his father and the Rabbi told them that everything we have, God has given to us. Where did you get your keenness of mind? Where did you get that strength of body that enables you to get up out of bed each morning and work hard all day? Did you put the oil in the rocks or the fertility in the soil or the fish in the sea? Do you remember Joyce Kilmer? "Poems are made by fools like me, but only God can make a tree." With all the people who have made a fortune in the lumber business, I wonder how many of them remember that? There is a famous chapter in the Book of Genesis, Chapter 22, which tells us about Abraham and his son, Isaac. Abraham was an old man. He was 100 years old and he wanted a son, and God gave him Isaac. And Isaac was the joy of his life. Now, God suddenly said to him, "I want you to sacrifice your son, your only son to me." And Abraham went out into the desert and was about to sacrifice his only son when the Angel of God stopped him. And then God said, "Because you were willing to do this, I swear, I will bless you abundantly." Is there some person in your life who brings you happiness and peace and serenity and love? Remember that person is God's gift to you in love. If God were to ask you to give that gift back, are you willing? This is a challenge we all have to face as we stand by the grave of a loved one who is called back to God. My dear friends, everything we have is God's gift to us. I remember reading about a district nurse who was very generous in her work. And the doctor said, "I'm going to ask for a raise for you. God knows you deserve it." And she said smiling, "If God knows, that's all that matters because I'm doing it all for Him." And I met a lady once who told me she had discovered the secret of happiness and radiant living. She said, "It is giving things away, tithing. Whenever I make extra money," she said, "I immediately give a tenth to the Church or to charity and I have such peace and serenity that I think Heaven has begun." There is the prayer of the famous St. Ignatius, the founder of the Jesuits, who said to God, "O Lord, I give you my memory, my understanding, my will. I give them all back to you who gave them to me. Do with them, as you will. In return all I ask you is that you give me your grace and your love. With these I am rich enough and ask for nothing more."

Three Things

Henry David Thoreau loved the simple life. For 17 years he lived in a cottage on Walden Pond in Concord. He expressed his philosophy like this, "I enjoy going to the town and visiting the stores and the marketplace and seeing all the things I don't need or want, that I can do without." Do you think some of us should use that philosophy? It is so easy to gather, to accumulate, and to hoard. Today's luxuries become tomorrow's necessities. At the end of the famous Thirteenth Chapter of First Corinthians, St. Paul tells us that there are three things that remain, three things that abide, three things that are necessary – faith, hope, and love. He said, "Without faith, it is impossible to please God." But, on a purely natural level one can say, without faith it is impossible to live. You and I could not get up in the morning without faith. To believe that the street is still there, that the streets are still there, that the job we work at is still there. My dear friend, without faith it would be impossible to start a business; or a person would need to have some ability and some capital. But unless they believed in themselves, they are doomed before they start. They must believe in their associates; they must believe in their employees; they must believe in the product they sell; they must believe in the public. And my dear friends, how is it possible to get an education without faith? You have to believe in the school that you choose, in the curriculum, in the integrity of the professors, in the authenticity of the authors of the books you study. Faith is absolutely imperative in life for all of us. But when it comes to the supernatural level, Our hidden God can be discovered only by faith and that was the great gift bestowed on you and me on the day we were baptized – that we have the power to believe, to accept, and to live our lives out on the conviction that Our God is Our Father who loves us. And hope – well, my dear friends, on the national level, an orderly peaceful life cannot be lived without hope. Look at the world around us. We are so dissatisfied with so much that is – there are so many wrongs that have not been righted, there is so much suffering that has not been alleviated, there is so much injustice that has not been rectified. And our own lives – we have problems without; we have failures within. We are not all that we should be or could be. We are hoping to improve. The current writing is not the final draft. I am hoping to grow in graciousness, hoping to lose my temper and my intolerance and my prejudice – I am hoping for this all the time. And on the supernatural level, as St. Augustine reminds us, "If my faith and my love is not fortified by hope, I am not complete. Oh my God, I hope in you for grace in this life and for glory in the life to come." And every morning at Mass we say, "…as we wait in hope for the coming of Our Lord Jesus Christ." The end of our lives will be the beginning of unending bliss promised by Him Who loves us – and that is our firm hope. And love, well, some of you, like myself, will remember Jeanette McDonald and Nelson Eddy singing, "Ah, sweet mystery of life, at last I've found you. Ah, at last I know the meaning of it all. Sure it's love and love alone the world is seeking." And then we have danced to the lovely melody, "I'll be loving you always, always, not for just a week, not for just a year, but always." And today young people are singing, "What the world needs now is love, sweet love. It's the only thing that there's just too little of." And they sing, "You are nobody 'til somebody loves you. You are nobody 'til somebody cares." But on the supernatural level, Our God's name is Love! His nature is love. He is loving you at this moment. It was His love that drew you out of nothingness in the yesteryears and His love has prepared an eternity of ecstasy for you. This is the God in Whom you and I must believe and hope and whom we are striving to love. So, let me pray the prayer we say at the beginning of Mass every day, "May the grace of Our Lord Jesus Christ and the love of God the Father and the fellowship of the Holy Spirit be with each one of you now and forever."

The Lord's Prayer

I am sure that over the years, you have come across collections of prayers – prayers of the ancients, prayers of the Irish, the *Oxford Book of Prayers*. They're all very interesting and very inspiring. But, of course, the prayer of prayers is the prayer taught us by Our Lord Jesus Christ that we say so often. Did you ever stop to think of the implication of that prayer? We say so easily "Our Father." God is the Father of us all, of course! But, my dear friend, much more importantly than that, He is the Father of you and the Jesus Christ

Who lives within you. Christ has brought the unending eternal life of God to you. It is flowing through your veins and beating next to your heart. Christ and you are so one that with St. Paul you can say, "I live now, no longer I, Christ lives in me." So that He is truly Your Father and you are talking to the Father in the name of Our Lord who said to you and me, "If you ask the Father anything in My Name, He will give it to you." And it is in His name you are saying the *Pater Noster*, and your Father and your God is in heaven. And where is heaven? Everywhere. God is everywhere. As St. Paul reminds us, "In Him we live and move and have our being." When I die, my soul will not take flight through Ireland on its way to Heaven. No, no, no. I will awaken to the reality that I have come here where I am now, the Lord living in me. We pray, "Your Kingdom come." May Christ come alive in me the way He has dreamed and planned from all eternity. Each one of us is going to have a likeness to Christ that no saint ever had or ever will have. And unless you and I correspond with the dream of the Lord, He will be disappointed forever. "Your will be done," by me today. St. Paul reminds us, this is the will of God – your sanctification, so that I may live today as a child of God in very truth with all the graciousness, with all the love, with all the understanding, with all the forgiveness that is now supposed to be in me become I am lifted up to Christ, grafted onto Him, the Vine. His will as it is in heaven. There is nothing in heaven but love. Our family who have gone before us are living every moment of love in heaven; and you and I are expected to live every moment of love on earth united with Our Elder Brother, the Lord Jesus Christ Who has been so good to us. We ask for our daily bread, that the Lord may give me the physical, emotional, and spiritual strength to live as His child today. Tragically, many of His children on this earth have no tangible bread to eat. They are starving in parts of the world. We who are so spoiled; but not on bread alone do we live and we ask Him to help us live a worthy life with Him, through Him, and in Him today. And teach us to forgive as graciously, as completely as He forgives us our stupid, selfish sins; that we may forgive the people who hurt us. And our hearts are small. Let's keep them small. Why do I magnify the trivia of the day and make myself measurable? Why don't I learn from Him how to forgive and how to forget? And I ask Him to lead me not into temptation but to deliver me from evil. He knows my weaknesses, my failings, my stupidities, my selfishness, my laziness, and my deafness. He knows my proclivities to evil better than I know them myself. And I ask Him to help me stay away from them all and stay close to Him.

Appealing Words

The most appealing words Our Lord ever used are in the Eleventh Chapter of St. Matthew's Gospel, "Come to me all you who labor and are heavily burdened and you will find rest for your souls. Learn of me for I am meek and humble of heart. My yoke is easy, my burden is light" (Matt. 12:29-30). Our Lord looked at the people around Him and saw they were fighting heavy battles and losing, and carrying great burdens but running out of strength. Sometimes life gets you and me down and there is tiredness, not of body but a weariness of soul that no amount of sleep can rectify. On such occasions we hear Him say, "Come to Me. Let Me help you carry your burden." Of course, sometimes the problem with us who know everything is that we are carrying burdens we were never intended to carry. The burdens and the problems belong to Him. He is in charge of the world; not you and I, and He can solve problems you and I could never solve. Do you remember when Moses met God in the burning bush? And Moses said to God, "What is Your Name? Whom shall I say sent me?" He said, "My Name is I AM." Not "I was," not "I will be." "I AM." God lives in the eternal now where there is neither past nor future. My dear friends, it is sobering to realize that at this very moment God sees you and me, not only on this lovely day that He has created, but He sees you and me already dead and buried and judged and safely home with Him forever in the ecstasy that He has planned for us. This He sees now. As you and I are here worrying and fretting about a future that may never come. But remember Moses was slow of speech. He stuttered and he stammered. He had an inferiority complex. And he said to God, "Who am I that, that, that I should go to the Pharaoh and tell him to let your people go?" And God said to him, "I shall be with you." And He was with Moses as He is with you and me. Moses believed that God would be with him. Do you and I? We say every day in the *Angelus*, "Behold the handmaid of the Lord. Be it done unto me according to Your Word." The words of Our Lady – She said them and She meant them. She had no idea what God had in store for Her. She could never in Her wildest dreams have imagined Bethlehem and the birth in the stable. Neither could She imagine the flight into Egypt and the long years of inactivity and waiting in Nazareth. But She allowed God to have His way with Her. "Behold the handmaid of the Lord. Be it done unto me according to Your Word." Can you and I say this and mean it? You see, my dear friends, we have to be reminded that God in His love has a plan for you and me, and that plan is filled with love. Our Lord said, "I am meek and humble of heart." He had no ego problems like we have. He was not looking for recognition or trying to impress anyone. My dear friend, the most difficult problem people have is preoccupation with self. To go into a room, to impress everybody there, and to come out wondering how you succeeded is wearing; it will exhaust you. The secret is to give yourself over to the Lord and He will take charge. And He asks us to link on to Him. The yoke is the piece of metal that links the two animals together. He wants us to work with Him in helping other human beings and there is nothing more salutary or more satisfying than to be able to help other people. My dear friend, it is not what happens to them when we help them; it's what happens to us when we give that help with the Lord. And surely, my dear friends, this is our prayer today, "O Lord, I thank You for all You have given me all my days when I was blinded by my selfishness and did not see Your love. I thank you now in anticipation for all you have planned for me in love and I accept now the death you have planned for me. Lord, You have no need of our praise; but our desire to thank you is itself your gift. Our prayer of thanksgiving adds nothing to your greatness but makes us grow in your grace through Jesus Christ Our Lord. In our joy we sing to your glory with all the choirs of angels as we hope we shall be singing with them for all eternity."

The Best is Yet to Be

"Grow old along with me! The best is yet to be, the last of life for which the first was made. Our times are in His Hand Who saith, 'A whole I planned, youth shows but half; Trust God: see all, nor be afraid!'" These words of the poet Robert Browning have been the philosophy of life for many people and are the philosophy of life for many people today. The trouble with us in this age is that we live in a youth-oriented culture. We have face-lifts and hair dyes and wrinkle-free creams and all kinds of cosmetics to keep us young; but that's an illusion. The clock finally catches up with us and we become old. Indeed, some of us are old. But, my dear friends, we use euphemisms like "senior citizens" and "golden age" but it doesn't work. My dear friends, I don't know why we camouflage this part of life which should be, ought to be, and is a wonderful time for so many people. It was for the two people in the Second Chapter of St. Luke's Gospel – Anna and Simeon. Anna was 84 years old. She had been married for seven years and had long since been a widow. Simeon was also an old man. The Holy Spirit told him that he would not see death until the Messiah came. And when the Child Jesus was offered in the Temple, he took Him in his arms and said, "Now You can dismiss your servant in peace, O Lord, for my eyes have seen the Salvation of Israel" (Luke 2:29-30). He was ready to die. They were wonderful people. Anna was full of life and vitality. She worked in the temple day and night. It is not true to say that old people become cranky. But alas, it is true to say that cranky people become old. Simeon and Anna were not living in the past – oh, they had moments of nostalgia, thinking of the happy days – but they were very much living in the future and in the present. As we say at Mass every day, "Waiting in joyful hope for the coming of Our Lord Jesus Christ." Over the years, I have worked very much with the Little Sisters of the Poor – angels of mercy, and kindness and love on this earth. They go around their nursing homes in their white habits, smilingly helping the older people whom God has entrusted to their care. And those older people are happy. You know, the sisters arrange plays in which the old people play parts, and they arrange concerts in which the old people participate. It is a joy to be with them. They are not sour old people. They are very confident; confident of God's love that sustains them. But, my dear friends, the living witness for all of us is our Holy Father Pope John Paul II. In spite of his Parkinson's Disease, in spite of his infirmities, look at his vitality. Look at the way he inspired the youth of the world in Toronto. Look at the way he goes to the ends of the earth to make Christ His Elder Brother known and loved. In his 80s he is very much alive and very youthful. Now, my dear friends, what was the secret for Anna and Simeon and for the Holy Father and for the wonderful men and women who live with the Little Sisters of the Poor? It is their relationship with their God. God is real to them, as He must become real to you and me. We have to remind ourselves that we are all of us on a journey, a journey home. Our home is not here. We are strangers; we are pilgrims; we are wanderers. Our home is with God in an unending ecstasy of bliss, which He has prepared for us. And as we are confident of that, then we have the peace and the serenity which is our birthright. The old hymn of Henry Lyte surely finds an echo in our heart this day, "Abide with me; fast falls the eventide. The darkness deepens; Lord with me abide. When other helpers fail and comforts flee, Help of the helpless, O abide with me. Swift to its close ebbs out life's little day; Earth's joys grow dim; its glories pass away. Change and decay in all around I see; O Thou who changest not, abide with me. Hold Thou Thy cross before my closing eyes; Shine through the gloom and point me to the skies. Heaven's morning breaks, and earth's vain shadows flee; In life, in death, O Lord, abide with me."

Are We Consistent?

In the Sixteenth Chapter of St. Luke, Our Lord tells an extraordinary story of a rich man and his manager. He discovered that the manager had been dishonest. So, he called him in to give an account of his stewardship. And the manager thought to himself, "I am too proud to beg and I am unable to dig ditches; so this is what I will do." And the first man, he came in. He said, "How much do you owe my master?" "One hundred barrels of wheat." "Make it fifty." The next one who came in, he said to him, "How much do you owe my master?" "One thousand bushels of oil." "Make it eight hundred." And Our Lord said, "The people of this world are much smarter in their dealings with each other than are the children of light." This man was a scoundrel; but he was a scoundrel all the way. His God was himself and his idea was financial security and he served himself well, all the way. My dear friends, what one has to say about this man and the people of the world, what Our Lord is trying to get over to us, is that they are consistent. Are we? We say we believe in God, not some vague deity above the clouds, but the God of Love; who took you and me out of nothingness in love; he came down and died for us in love; who sustains us in love; who has destined us for an eternity of love. Do we really believe in Him? When trouble comes, we wring our hands, we frown our brows, and we get sleepless nights and headaches. I like this little piece of Doggerel, "Said the sparrow to the robin, I'd really like to know, why these anxious human beings, rush about and worry so. Said the sparrow to the robin, Friend I think that it must be; that they have no Heavenly Father, such as cares for you and me.' " In the Official Thanksgiving of the priest after Mass every morning, there is the use of the *Canticle of Daniel*. Daniel calls on all creation to praise and worship God – the sun, the moon and the stars, the valleys, and the hills. And then there is this line, "Let every bird in the sky bless the Lord." Outside my window in New York where I live, birds fly by very often. And sometimes one will alight on my windowsill and peck the glass in the window to remind me – "We neither sow nor spin nor gather into barns and Our Heavenly Father takes care of us. How much more will He take care of you?" We say we believe in eternity; but don't we live as if time were to go on forever? One thinks of the Little Flower saying that she had never been more than three minutes in her own life when she was not thinking of Our Lord with Whom she was going to spend her eternity. And then we say we believe in people, that every one of us is a child of God, that we are going to be together in Paradise. How do we treat people, as our brothers and sisters in the Lord? Remember, He told us, what we do to them, we do to Him. Sometimes we don't like others because of our sophistication, because of their background, because of their lack of education. My dear friends, we say that we believe in spiritual values, that it isn't what we have but what we are inside. And look at the way we go to the mall and spend money and buy material things. Where is our conviction? Where is our consistency? Well, my dear friends, all we can do is keep trying. Begin again. And the poem, the psalm that we say after Mass every day is surely true. "O God, You are My God. For You I long; for You my soul is thirsting; my body pines for You like a dry and weary land without water. So, I gaze on You in the sanctuary. For Your love is better than life. On my bed, I remember You. On You I muse through the night. For You have been my help. In the shadow of Your wings I rejoice. My soul clings to You. Your right hand holds me fast."

BONUS – ADDITIONAL THOUGHTS

God Lives Within You

On a Sunday morning, we all stand and make our Profession of Faith. "We believe in One God, the Father, the Almighty, Maker of Heaven and Earth, of all that is seen and unseen." And this is not a prayer. This is a statement of fact. This is our conviction. Like David in Psalm 23 when he said, "The Lord is My Shepherd, there is nothing I shall want. The Lord is the light of my countenance; of whom should I be afraid?" Why are we so convinced, you and I? Because the God gave us, when we were baptized, the breathtaking, extraordinary gift of faith to accept that Christ is God, that His Word is true, and that you and I are able to dedicate ourselves to Him and live out our lives on His Word. This is God's gift to us. Let us think about it in this fashion: In the last century, there was an Englishman, Edward Bulwer-Litton, who wrote a play called *The Cardinal*, and a line from that play has endured through the years. "The pen is mightier than the sword." We know that ideas rule the world. We are told there is nothing more powerful on earth than an idea whose time has come. Henry Ford got the idea of the mass production of the automobile; today the world is on wheels. Louis Pasteur, the French scientist, got the idea that heat destroys germs. Today all our milk is pasteurized. Is there any idea in our religion, any idea from the Gospels whose time has come? Is there any idea that will help the frightened teenager on the threshold of life, who wants to escape from the challenge in drink, drugs or suicide? Any idea to help the shattered young woman when the man to whom she has given the best years of her life, given her youth and her dreams and her love, walks out and leaves her to rear the children alone? And she knows now that like her Lord and Master, she too has been betrayed by a kiss. Any idea that will help the brokenhearted widow or widower standing at the grave's edge when all their love has been put six feet under; and now, they must pick up the pieces and begin again, alone. Any idea that will help you and me, as we go on our unremembered way down here in this valley of tears, trying to give our lives a meaning. Is there any idea from the Gospel? Oh yes, there is. The most potent, the most revolutionary idea the world has ever known. The sad part is that you and I have grown up with it. Listen to the words of Our Lord now from the Fifteenth Chapter of St. John's Gospel as if you never heard them before – as if they were being uttered on this earth for the first time and spoken to you personally. "I am the vine and you are the branches. Live in me so that I, Your God, can live in you" (John 15:5). And listen to His Words in the Sixth Chapter of St. John's Gospel. "Unless you eat the Flesh of the Son of Man and drink His Blood, you shall not have life in you. He who eats My Flesh and drinks My Blood has eternal life, and I shall raise him up on the last day" (John 6:53-54). These are extraordinary words that you and I need to hear again, again and again. My dear friends, whoever you are listening to me, sitting there now with a thousand stray thoughts on your mind, with your worries and your fears and your insecurities, you don't need to be told by me, because you have been tutored by the years, the same as I have. It is not easy to be a creature. To be a creature is, by definition, to be alone. Each one of us is a unique creation of God. Each one of you listening to me now inhabits the world, the silent world of your own fear, your own loneliness, your own fascination with evil, that no one, no one can see or understand. Each one of you has your own individual history behind you and your own unique destiny awaiting you, which you cannot share with any human being. One day, you will die – alone. You were born – alone. And in the last analysis, however close you may be to your family and to your friends, you are essentially alone. As Bishop Sheen liked to remind young lovers, that one and one would always remain. To be a creature means to be in time and to be of time. The moment the umbilical cord was cut, you and I were flung into the river of time and that river is floating onward relentlessly, moment-by-moment, and there is nothing you and I can do about it. We can't organize a protest swim against the tide, or raise our puny fists in defiance. And look at what time has done to us. And to be a creature means to be restless. I'm always trying to escape from the present moment. It's so drab; it's so dreary. I'm always putting something on the horizon. I'm always looking forward; I'm always looking into the future in my dreams, in my imaginings. The things I want, I cannot have; the things I have seem out of date; the things I want to do, I can't; the things I have to do, I hate. That's us - restless creatures. And then, to be a creature means to be afraid. We are afraid of the dark; we are afraid of the unknown; we are afraid of the future; we are afraid of losing our family and friends; we are afraid of sickness; we are afraid of old age; we are afraid of death and we are scared of the thought of what comes after death. Don't you remember Shakespeare? "To sleep, perchance to dream...What dreams may come when we have shuffled off this mortal coil must give us pause....The undiscovered country from whose bourn no traveler returns....makes us rather bear those ills we have than fly to others that we know not of? Thus conscience does make cowards of us all..." No, it is not easy to be a creature and to inhabit my own world, alone. Now, the mystery of Christ Who is God is that He has come into this world that is you and I. He has come to live there, to share our loneliness, our challenge, and our fears, to give us strength to meet the challenge of every hour. You remember Claire Booth Luce? She was that extraordinary Connecticut Yankee. She was a Congresswoman; she was a playwright; she was a leader of fashion; she was America's ambassador to Italy. She wrote wonderfully. She was married to Henry Luce, the publisher of *Life* magazine. She had lots of money. She had a daughter whom she worshipped. The world was her oyster. One day, her only child, her daughter, was killed in an accident. Her world came crashing down about her ears. Everything was dark and dreary and dismal. There was no reason to get up in the morning now. She went into a deep depression. Her friends tried to console her, and to support her, but to no use. Finally, someone told her about Bishop Sheen, that she ought to go and talk to him. She did. And she listened to him. And she was baptized a Catholic. A few months after her Baptism, daring woman that she was, she gave a lecture at The Catholic University in Washington. And she stood there before the assembled student body and the faculty, and she said, "Would someone define a 'Catholic'? What does it mean to be a Catholic?" And she gave her own definition. I doubt you can improve on it. She said, "A Catholic is someone to whom, when a stranger comes up in the street merely to ask you the time of day, the stranger should be able to tell from the tone of your voice, from the smile on your lips, from the gleam in your eye, that the Lord lives within you." Have you made that discovery, you who are listening to me now? Do you realize, whoever you are, however weak or wayward or wicked, that the God with Whom you are going to spend eternity has come down and is living in you, in the depths of your being, nearer to you than you are to yourself? This is breathtaking! Listen to St. Paul in his Third Chapter of Colossians. "God's plan is this: to make known His secret to His people, this rich and glorious secret which He has for all peoples. And the secret is this: Christ is in you, which means that you share the glory of God" (Col. 3:14-15). He's in you at this moment, to share your loneliness, your sorrow, your sense of failure, your inability to cope – whatever it is, you are not alone. You are not lost in the crowd; you are not a number; you are not a cipher. You are someone loved by God passionately; loved so much that He is there in the depths of your being, as St. Augustine said, "...nearer to you than you are to yourself." "I am the place where God shines through for He and I are one, not two. I need not fret, nor fear, nor plan. He wants me where I am. And if I be relaxed and free, He'll carry out His plan through me." And Sr. Mary Ignatius, one morning after Holy Communion wrote, "It's this that makes my spirit spin – that Heaven is not up, but in." Where God is, Heaven is. St. Augustine in his famous *Confessions* understood so clearly the meaning and the mystery of Christianity.

"Too late have I known You, O Everlasting Truth. Too late have I loved You, O Beauty always old and ever new. Behold, You were within and I looked for you elsewhere, and in my weakness, I ran after the beauty of the things that you have made. You were in me

and I was not with you. The things you created kept me far from you. You have called; you have cried out, and have pierced my deafness. You have shone forth and have lifted my blindness. You have sent forth your sweetness and I have longed after you and looked for you. I have tasted you and now my great hope is in nothing else but in your great mercy, O Lord, My God. For he does not love you who loves anything else which he does not love for your sake. O love which always burns and never grows less, true charity, my God, set me all on fire. Give me what you command and command what you wish. All-powerful God, You care for each one of us as if you looked on us alone, and you care for all as if all were one. Things of this world pass away that others may replace them, but you never pass away or never depart. O God Our Father, supremely good, beauty of all things beautiful, to you we entrust whatsoever we have received from you through Jesus Christ, Our Lord."

My dear friends, practically it means today is all you and I have – this day that the Lord wants you – and we are talking about you – to be aware of Him. You and He together, the two of *you*, that you will laugh and weep together, whether you eat or drink, whatever else you do, that you will do it together, the Lord and you. St. Francis, the founder of the Franciscan order to which I belong, had a prayer which we say every day. Surely it is our prayer now. "O great and glorious God, and My Lord Jesus Christ, enlighten, I beseech you, the darkness of my mind. Give me a right faith, a firm hope, and a perfect charity. Grant that I may know You, O Lord, so that always and in all things, I may act in accord to Your Most Holy and Perfect will."

Our Hope is in You, O Lord

In 19th Century England, there was a famous convert, Frederick William Faber. He became a priest of the Oratory in London, in Brampton Oratory. His wonderful books were the bedside reading of Pope John XXIII. In one of his books, *The Creator and the Creature*, he wrote, "There are some thoughts which, however old they are, are always new, either because they are so broad that we never entirely learn them or because they are so intensely practical that their interest is always absorbing." And such thoughts are, for the most part, very common thoughts. They require no peculiar keenness of vision, for no one can fail to perceive them. They are like the huge mountains visible to everybody on the plain below. Now, among such thoughts we may reckon that thought which every child knows – that God loves each one of us with a special love. That God loves each one of you listening to me now with a special love, as if you were the only human being on earth. From all eternity – from all eternity, God determined to create you. Not just another soul, the child of your parents, an additional child to live in the 20th century, but He resolved to create you, just as you are – you, different from all people who ever existed or ever will exist. You who can be recognized as different, you who will answer to a name. You who have got a set of fingerprints that are not found anywhere else on this earth. And remember, God never had to create you. Never! Millions of possible uncreated beings that God saw when he created you, He left to remain in their nothingness. And they might have worshipped Him a thousand times better than you would ever worship Him. They might have been higher, holier, far more interesting. But He did not create them. There was some nameless thing about you, which attracted Him. It was you with your single unmated soul, which in the calmness of His eternal wisdom and love drew Him to create you. This is our faith. And my dear friend, that love of God never leaves you. The love that took you out of nothingness in the yesteryears did not put you into this world and leave you here on your own to sink or swim. That love has supported you and enveloped you every single moment since then. The next breath you draw, the next beat of your heart, is an act of God's love for you. Were He to cease to love you for one instant, you would cease to be. That is how close He is. That is how dependent you and I are on the God Who created us and is continuing to create us. Sometimes you may have seen the slogan on a car, "God is not finished with me yet." This is literally true. God is continuing to create you and me in love, even though we are not aware of it, every moment. You and I forget Him. He never for one instant forgets us. You and I stop loving Him. But He never for an instant ceases to love us. This is our faith. Now, my dear friends, Faith, Hope, and Love are variations on a theme. The God Who created me in love and sustains me in love and has destined me for an eternity in love, I accept that; I believe that. So, logically, I trust the God Who made me, on whom I am dependent. St. Augustine reminds us that the Christian soul that is not alive with hope, as well as with faith and love, is not complete. Have you made an "Act of Hope" recently? "O My Lord, I hope in you for grace in this life and for glory in the life to come, because you promised it, and unlike us, you never break Your Word. You never go back on your promise. I hope in You, O God, because of your mercy, which is above all of your works, which is not put off by my laziness, by my stupidity, by my sins. And I hope in You, O God, because of your power which can do all things, even with me." There is a line in the Third Chapter of St. Paul's Epistle to the Ephesians that you and I should write down in gold in our hearts – in gold because gold never tarnishes. "He whose power is at work in us is powerful enough and more than powerful enough to achieve His designs, beyond all our hopes and our dreams." He Whose power is at work in you, listening to me now – the Holy Spirit, God's Power, God's Wisdom, God's Love - is powerful enough and more than powerful enough to achieve His designs – not yours, not mine – His designs. Because God put you and me on this earth with some work to do that no one else can do. And He is going to achieve that design beyond all our hopes and dreams. My dear friends, you and I must take large draughts of hope. The cry is made to all Christians, "Thou shalt not despair!" Of all the grave sins that you and I could commit, despair is the gravest, because there is no soul this side of the grave beyond redemption – no soul. Our Lord died for every human being He created. There is no one, howsoever tortured or twisted, who cannot be flooded with peace by the Almighty. And there is no one howsoever low that cannot be lifted to the greatest heights by the God whose name is Love. And we have seen this time and time again in the history of sinners who became great saints. But my dear friends, the supernatural virtue of Hope that was given to you and me at our Baptism with Faith and Love, has to do with God, and the things of God, and the eternal life that is destined for us. My dear friends, we are on a journey. We are pilgrims, we strangers. Sometimes we are aware of this when illness strikes, when some tragedy occurs, when there is some great disappointment – we are made suddenly aware that life is really not what we thought it was. Cardinal Newman wrote his own epitaph: *Ex ombres et imaginibus in veritatem* which means "From the shadows and the images into the truth." My dear friend, when the next millennium dawns, you and I will be with God in eternity. Do you ever think about Heaven? That is your home. St. Paul almost defies us. He says, "Eye has not seen, nor ear heard, nor the heart of man been able to conceive what things God has prepared for those who love Him." "Eye has not seen, nor ear heard, nor the heart of man been able to conceive what things God has prepared..." for you, listening to me now. My dear friend, doesn't it sound like poetry or rhetoric to say that your place is ready in Heaven? He told us, "I have gone to prepare a place for you so that where I am, you also may be." And remember, from all eternity, not just in time, God loved you and created a place for you with Him in Heaven. And a thousand times today your guardian angel has passed by that place and seen your name there, and prayed God that nothing would so distract you or so absorb you or so turn your head down here as to make you forget the end for which you were created – to see God face-to-face, to occupy that place, that throne in glory for endless ages, where there will be no sorrow, no tears, no disappointment, no failure, where all your dreams now will have been realized in ways you and I cannot even begin to imagine, and that you will be with Your God. Now, dear friend, do you realize that you and I are not going to Heaven? No, we are not. We cannot go to Heaven because Heaven has come to us. Where God is, Heaven is. And where God comes to you and me in Holy Communion, Heaven is there in the depth of our being. And in faith, I have but to enter the sanctuary of my baptized soul where My God lives and taste in anticipation something of the joy and fulfillment and happiness that awaits me. No wonder St. Catherine of Siena cried out, "All the way to Heaven is Heaven because of Him Who is the Way living in me." My dear friend, how we thank Him for our faith and for our hope, that when you and I close our eyes on this world, we will open them to reality. We will discover then what Cardinal Newman discovered – that all this about images and shadows, the real world where God lives, is already within you and me. Eternal life was planted in us the day you and I were baptized. And when we die, we shall simply open our eyes to the reality that we have become. There was a great Franciscan in the Middle Ages, Duns Scotus, a Scot, who was a great lover of Our Lady and a great lover of Her Son. He's buried in the cathedral of Cologne, in Germany, and on his tombstone is written these little words, in Latin: *Semel sepultus bis mortuus, "He was buried once. He died twice."* He died to the things of this world before he closed his eyes in death. He realized that all that he saw was unreal in comparison with the reality of eternal life, and he was wise enough to become detached from the world. So must you. So must I. Our problem, God help us, poor creatures that we are, is that like St. Augustine, we fall in love with the gifts of God. We become enamored with the beauty of the world around us, all created by God, and we forget the Endless Beauty, the Creator. St. Francis died at 45, and he was able to say, "My God and My All." God was everything for him. In your own way and in my own way, we have to detach ourselves and disentangle ourselves and disengage ourselves from people who mean so much to us, from the things that God has given to us for which we are so grateful, and fix our gaze on Him, on Him alone with Whom we are going to spend our eternity. In the famous suite of music, *Finlandia*, by Sibelius, after very tortuous passages, there comes a very beautiful melody, and the words of an 18th-century hymn are used in that melody. I think these words are very beautiful because they are very true. "Be still, my soul. The Lord is on thy side. Bear patiently the cross of grief or pain. Leave to Thy God to order and provide, who faithful is and faithful will remain. Be still my soul, thy best, thy changeless friend through thorny waves leads to a joyful end."

Becoming Who You Love

Nathaniel Hawthorne has a wonderful story about a boy who lived in a village. Across from the village was a mountain, in which he could see so clearly etched in stone, the features of a human being. And he wondered whose face it was in the mountain. He looked at everyone in the village, but no one resembled the face in the mountain. Whenever a stranger came to town, he looked steadily at them to see if they were the face in the mountain. But no one was the face in the mountain. And the story ends by telling us, as the boy grew into manhood, he became the face in the mountain. He looked at it so long, so intently; he actually came to resemble it. And this is a natural phenomenon. People become like whom they love. A man has some peculiarity of speech; his wife unconsciously acquires the same. Or she walks in some strange way, and finally, so does he. My dear friends, the whole challenge of your life and mine is to look at Christ, Our Elder Brother, so long, so lovingly, that eventually He and we become one. And it is not that I imitate Christ from a distance, oh no. It is that I bring the Christ already living in me alive in very truth. The famous prayer of Cardinal Newman he calls *My Prayer*: "Dear Jesus, help me to spread your fragrance everywhere I go. Flood my soul with your spirit and life, penetrate and possess my whole being so utterly, that all my life may be only a radiance of Thine. Shine through me and be so in me that every soul I come in contact with may feel your presence in my soul. Let them look up and see, no longer me, but only Jesus. The light, O Lord, will be only from you, none of it will be mine." Our Lord said, "I have come that you might have life and have it to the full. I am the Life." And St. Paul boasted, "I live, no longer I, but Christ lives in me." Now, Christ Our God has come down to show you and me how to live. He is our model in living, and He is in us in His Spirit to enable us to bring Him alive. This is the meaning of our religion. Fr. Walter Burkhart, the great contemporary preacher in America, has written a book. He calls it *Dare to Be Christ*. Now, St. Paul tells us in his Chapter Thirteen of First Corinthians, "There is faith, hope and love, but the greatest of these is love" (1 Cor. 13:3). And love is simply Christ, because God is Love. Christ alive in human beings, and that is you listening to me and me talking to you. And St. Paul says, "Even if I speak with the tongues of men and of angels and have not love, I am nothing. Even if I give away all my goods to feed the poor, and my body to be burnt at the stake and have not love, I am only a tinkling brass or a clanging cymbal" (1 Cor. 13:1-3). It means nothing. St. Augustine summed it all up. He said, "Love, and do what you like." When you and I do what we do with Christ, through Christ and in Christ who is Love, then we understand the challenge. But my dear friends, the word "love" is so often misunderstood. It is not just the romantic love that a man has for a maid, or the inspiring love that, you know, a friend has for a friend, or the wonderful love that a mother has for a child. No, it is God's Own Love, given to you and me as His children that we must use and live and show to the world. And St. Paul defines it in the Thirteenth Chapter of First Corinthians. "Love is patient, it is kind, it feels no envy, and it is never perverse or proud. It does not brood over an injury. It takes no pleasure in wrongdoing, but it rejoices at the victory of truth. It

163

sustains; it hopes; it endures to the end" (1 Cor. 13:4-7). "Love is patient." How patient are we, you and I? Oh, of course we're patient. We're civilized; we're disciplined; we are controlled. We do not explode in public. We wait until we come home. I don't punch you in the nose in anger. I reserve that and punch the pillow when I get home before I go to bed. My dear friends, Our Lord showed us patience in action. He was lied about; He was misunderstood; He was spat upon; He was mocked; He was derided; He was led like a sheep to the slaughter, opening not His mouth. But you're saying, "Oh, my dear Franciscan unenlightened priest, I'm only a human being. I don't have that kind of love." Oh, but my dear friends listening to me, of course you do, because if you have Christ living within you, you have His patience there in the depth of your own being. When you and I receive Him in Holy Communion, He communicates to us everything He has. You and I have His patience. The problem is, I don't like the challenge. It's too much and I'm too lazy. I have my own brand of patience, inferior, shoddy, the kind that is limited and that runs out. I have the patience of the Lord. I am standing on a spiritual gold mine. He has given me the pearl of priceless value. I never use it. Oh, I worship Him with prayers. I give Him lip service, but I do not honor Him with my heart. And the proof is, I do not use His patience, which He has given to me. And His kindness – how kind are we? Oh, we are kind, of course. We had a good mother. But, my dear friends, does our kindness depend on the state of our health or the weather or the time of day? Before coffee in the morning, I'm not too sweet. Or does it depend on the people around me, how kind they are to me? Remember Our Lord showing forth His kindness. He was kind to sinners who hated Him. He was kind to mothers who can be so demanding. He was kind to children who can be so exasperating. He was kind to the sick that can be so unreasonable. He was always kind. The French say, "In order to be kind enough, we must be too kind. In order to be kind enough, we must be too kind." Do you think we are too kind? My dear friends, when you and I look at a crucifix and hear Our Lord say, "Greater love than this no one has, than to lay down one's life for one's friends," He was being too kind. St. Vincent DePaul gives one formula for sanctity, "Be kind; be kind and you will be a saint." That sounds easy, doesn't it? Oh, to be kind to the haughty and to the selfish and the demanding and the ungrateful, those who squander my kindness and never say "thank you," and then come back for more. In order to be kind like this, I have to be very united with My Lord. Isn't this the way He's treated by all of us? Outside the door now, people are going by in cars. Their next breath comes from Him, in love. The next beat of their heart comes from Him in love. Do they thank Him? They take it all for granted. No wonder we have in the Church contemplative nuns and monks who spend their lives trying to prove to the Lord that He was not a fool, that it was not wasted, that they, at least, are interested and grateful in the name of the rest of us. And in Christ, there is no envy. Envy? Why should I be envious? What was the greatest thing that happened to the Holy Father this morning? He received Our Lord in Holy Communion. So did I! And I have to spend this day meeting the challenge of keeping Him alive. I don't have time to be envious. Do you ever watch musicians in an orchestra playing as they are involved and dedicated so seriously? The violinist is not envious of the cellist, and the trombonist is not envious of the flautist. Each is making music, each in his own way. And you and I, each of us, have something to do for God on this earth that no one else can do. So, I must be busy doing my job, living my life where He has placed me. I don't have time to be looking at you or studying you, envious of you. Remember, my dear friends, we didn't ask to be born in the twentieth or the twenty-first century. He arranged it all in love. We are not living in the year 1799, or 1899, or 2099. We are living in this year of grace, given a challenge that will never come again, and we must be busy meeting the challenge every hour of every day with Him Who lives in us. And there is no pride. Pride? My dear friend, why should I be proud and of what? Everything I have He has given to me – everything. And my dear friend, you, whoever you are, listening to me now, everything you have, He has given to you – your health, your happiness, your profession, your success, your family, everything, everything He has given to you in love. The only thing God has not given to you and me are our sins. These are all I can call my own – my selfishness, my failure to appreciate His goodness, my lack of awareness of Him, my superficiality, my arrogance – these are mine. Everything else is His. Do you remember in Shakespeare's play *Henry VIII*, Cardinal Woolsey, an old and broken man, cried out, "I have ventur'd like little wanton boys who swim on bladders this many summers in a sea of glory, but far beyond my depth: my high-blown pride at length broke under me; and now has left me, weary and old with service, to the mercy of a rude stream, that must forever hide me...Had I but served my God with half the zeal I served my king, He would not in mine age have left me naked to mine enemies." And look what a fierce zeal we bring to the service of our ego, of our importance, our work, our profession, our popularity, our fame. If only we had served Our God with half the zeal we served ourselves. There is no pride in love. There is only humility and gratitude and spiritual ambition. And love never falls away. It never changes. Love has only one mood – constant, unchanging, everlasting. Our Lord's actions proved this to us. I wonder how you and I would treat someone who doubted our word. Oh, such an insult, to doubt my word! Someone who denied me, was ashamed of me – well, the back of 'me hand to them. Or someone who betrayed me with a kiss of friendship and sold me for thirty pieces of silver – would I still call them "friend" as Our Lord called Thomas and Peter and Judas? We have much learning to do, all of us, before we get to Heaven. Because, my dear friends, when you and I die, if we have not graduated *summa cum laude* in love, we cannot enter Heaven. There's nothing there but love, and all my days, I must strive to learn to love. One thinks of what a marvelous human being Our Lady must have been. Imagine having Her as a neighbor, living down the street, Her smile, Her welcome, and so genuine. And you never intruded; you were never an interruption; it was never an inopportune time. And you could borrow the sugar or milk or money and forget to return it and you were still welcome. And Her listening ear, and whatever you told Her, no one ever heard. It is no wonder the Protestant, Wordsworth, called Mary, "Our tainted nature's solitary boast." - The mother and the Son. Well, my dear friends, it is easy to talk. But surely the prayer of St. Ignatius, the great founder of the Jesuits, is our prayer this day. "Teach me, My God, to be generous. Teach me to love and serve you as you deserve; to give and not to count the cost; to fight and not to heed the wound; to toil and not to seek for rest; to labor and to look for no reward except your love."

Get the Complete Collection!

Fr. Leo Clifford was one of the Church's most gifted and distinguished speakers. These Reflections air daily on EWTN and are also available on DVD/CD. Each Volume is approximately 90 minutes.

FR. LEO CLIFFORD'S REFLECTIONS

VOLUME I
Item #: HDR1 - DVD
Item #: HCR1 - CD
VOLUME II
Item #: HDR2 - DVD
Item #: HCR2 - CD
VOLUME III
Item #: HDR3 - DVD
Item #: HCR3 - CD
VOLUME IV
Item #: HDR4 - DVD
Item #: HCR4 - CD
VOLUME V
Item #: HDR5 - DVD
Item #: HCR5 - CD

$15 each

BOOK & DVD SET OF 5 VOL
- $65.00
ITEM#: HDRSET

BOOK & CD SET OF 5 VOL
- $65.00
ITEM#:HCRSET

BOOK *- $12.00*
ITEM#: 51200

To place an order or to see more great products from EWTN Home Video, go to: ewtnrc.com